My Pacific Northwest Favorites

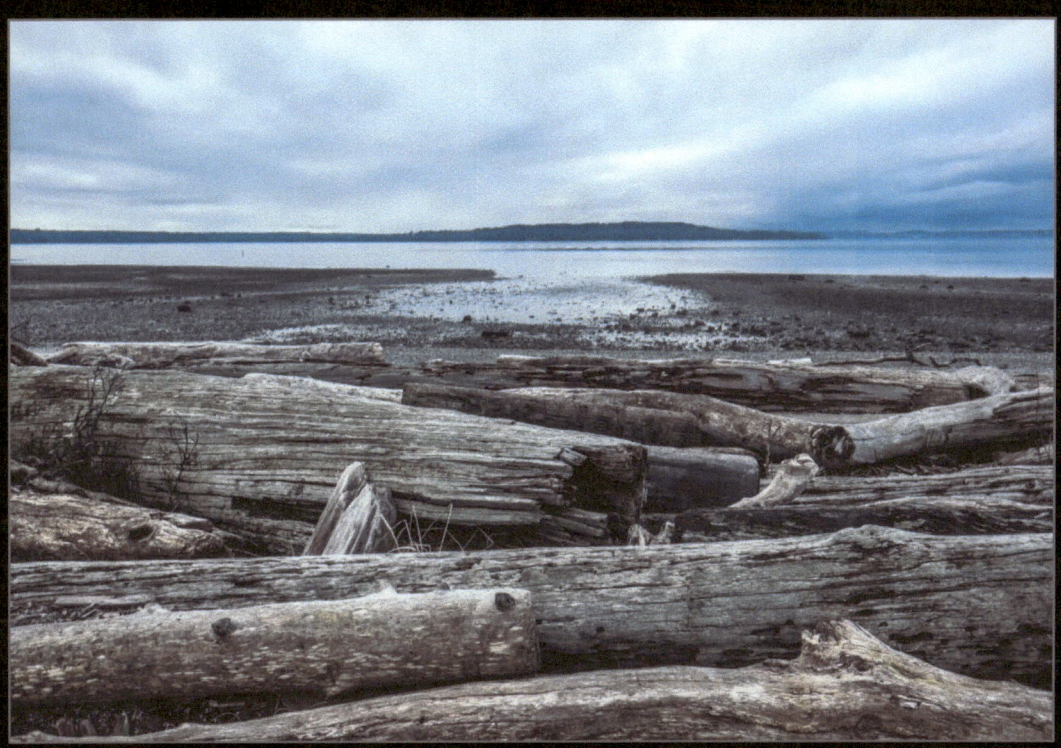

George Matthew Cole

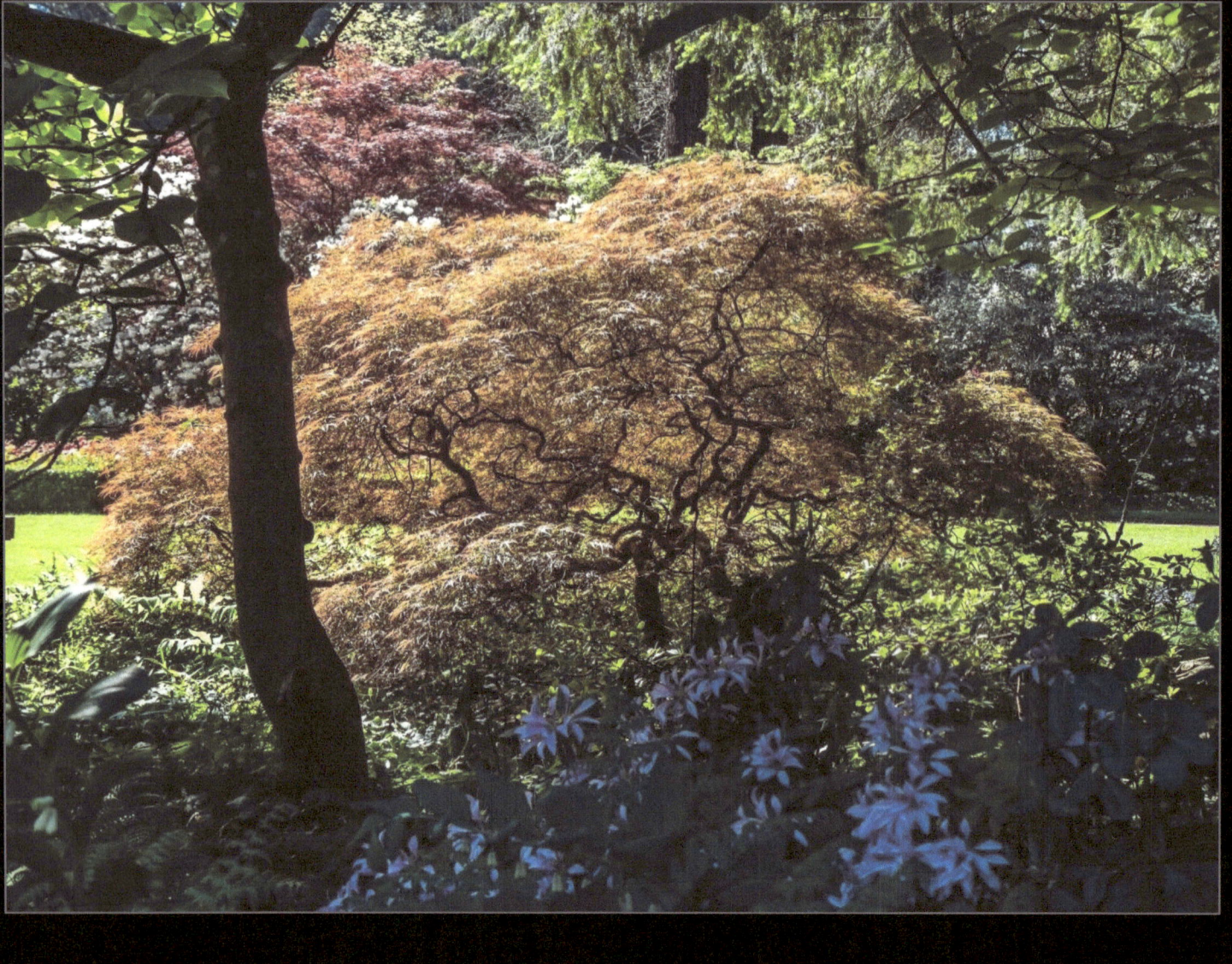

Vibrant golden leaves grow
on this Japanese Maple
tree in a garden.

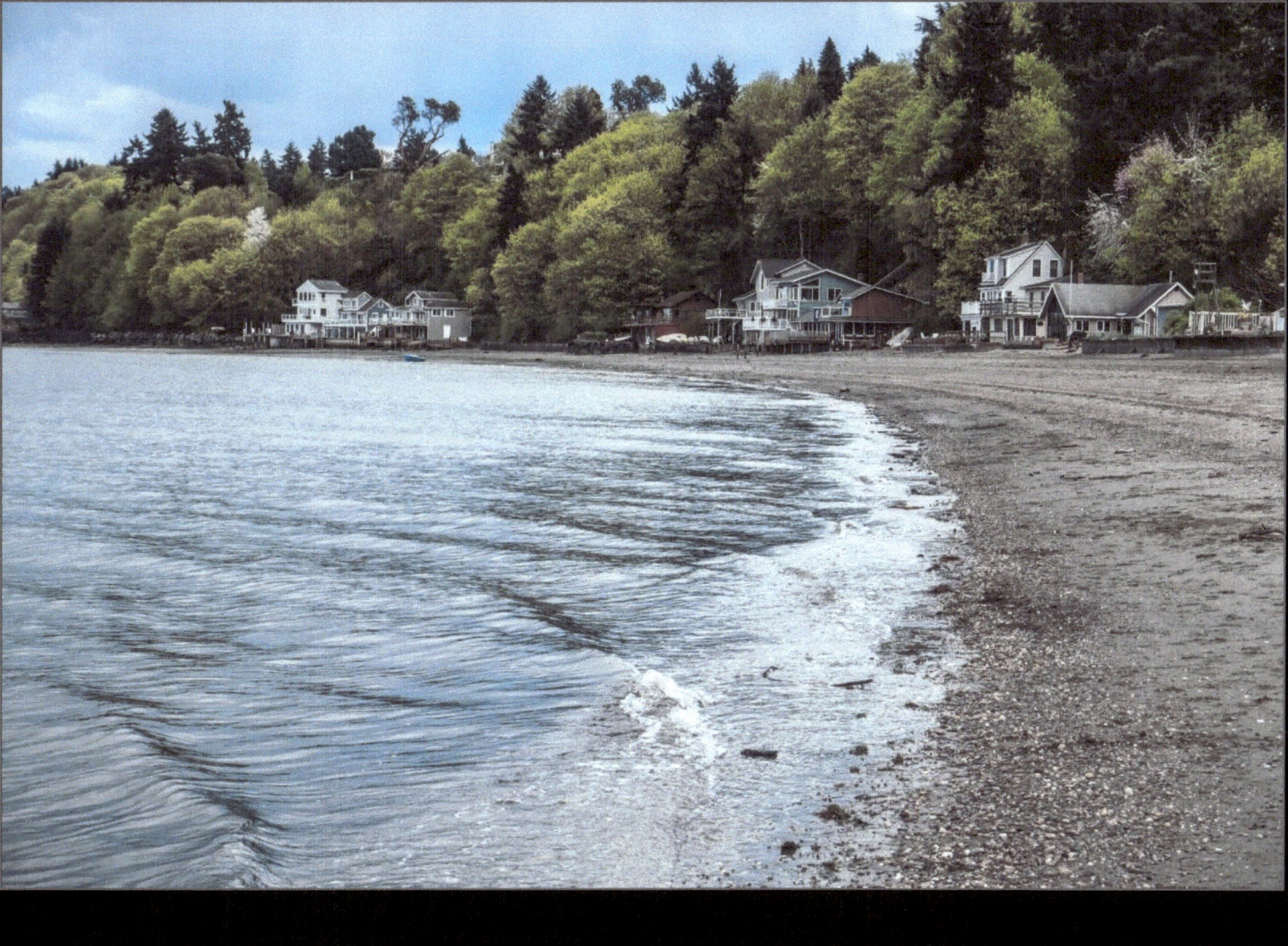

Waterfront homes are nestled under

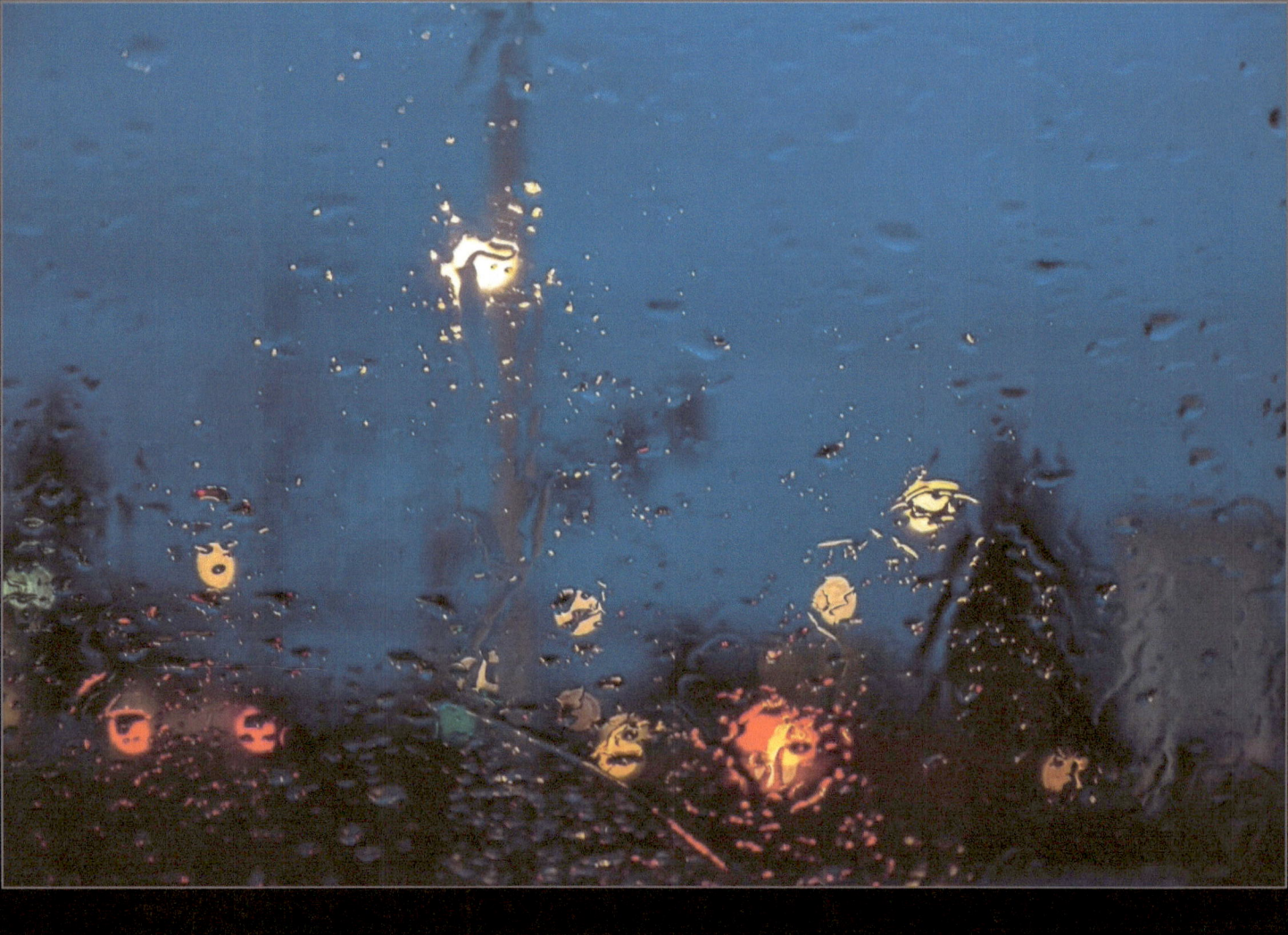

Raindrops on a car windshield create

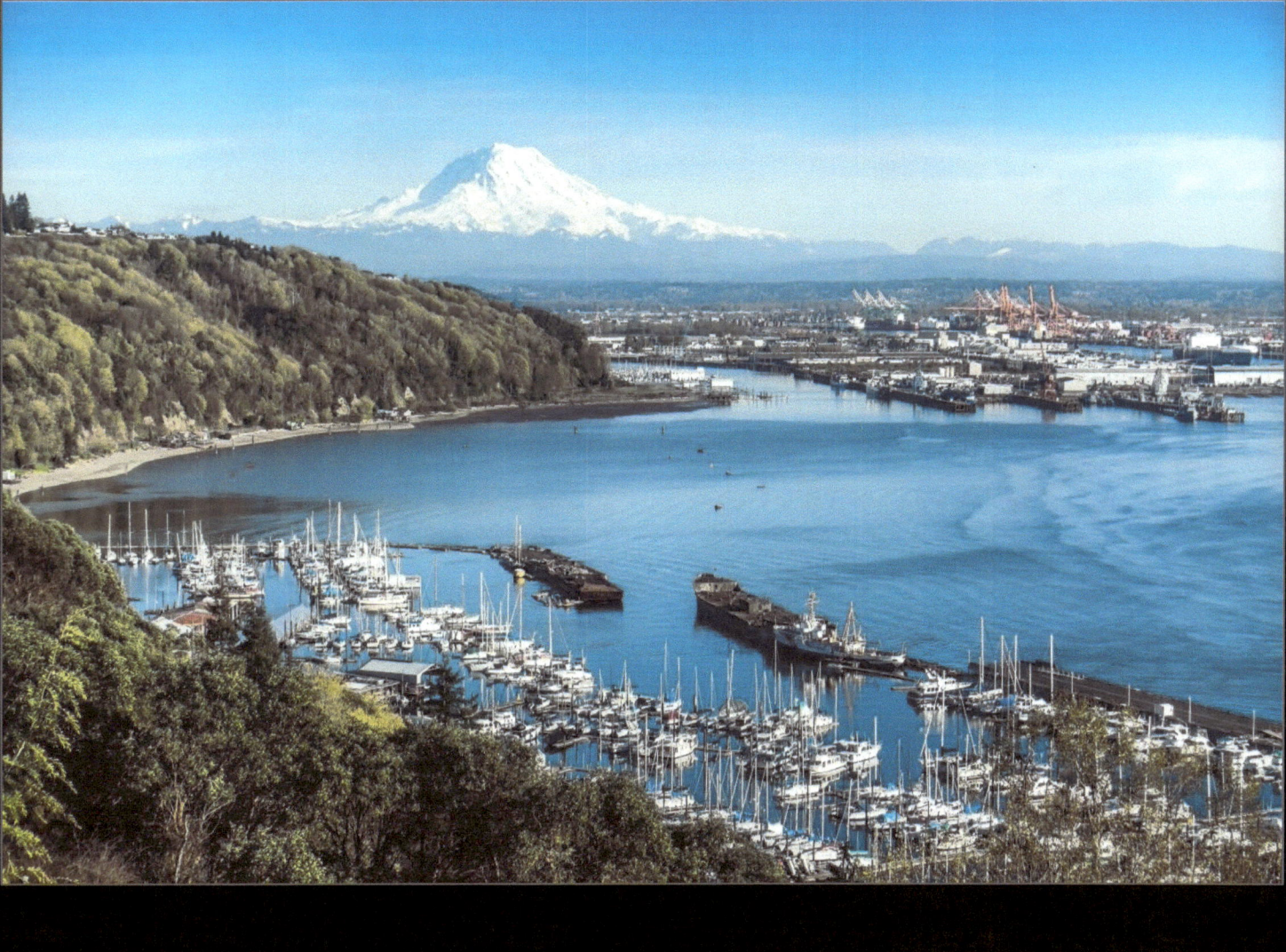

Majestic Mount Rainier rises above
the Port of Tacoma with sailboats
moored at a marina.

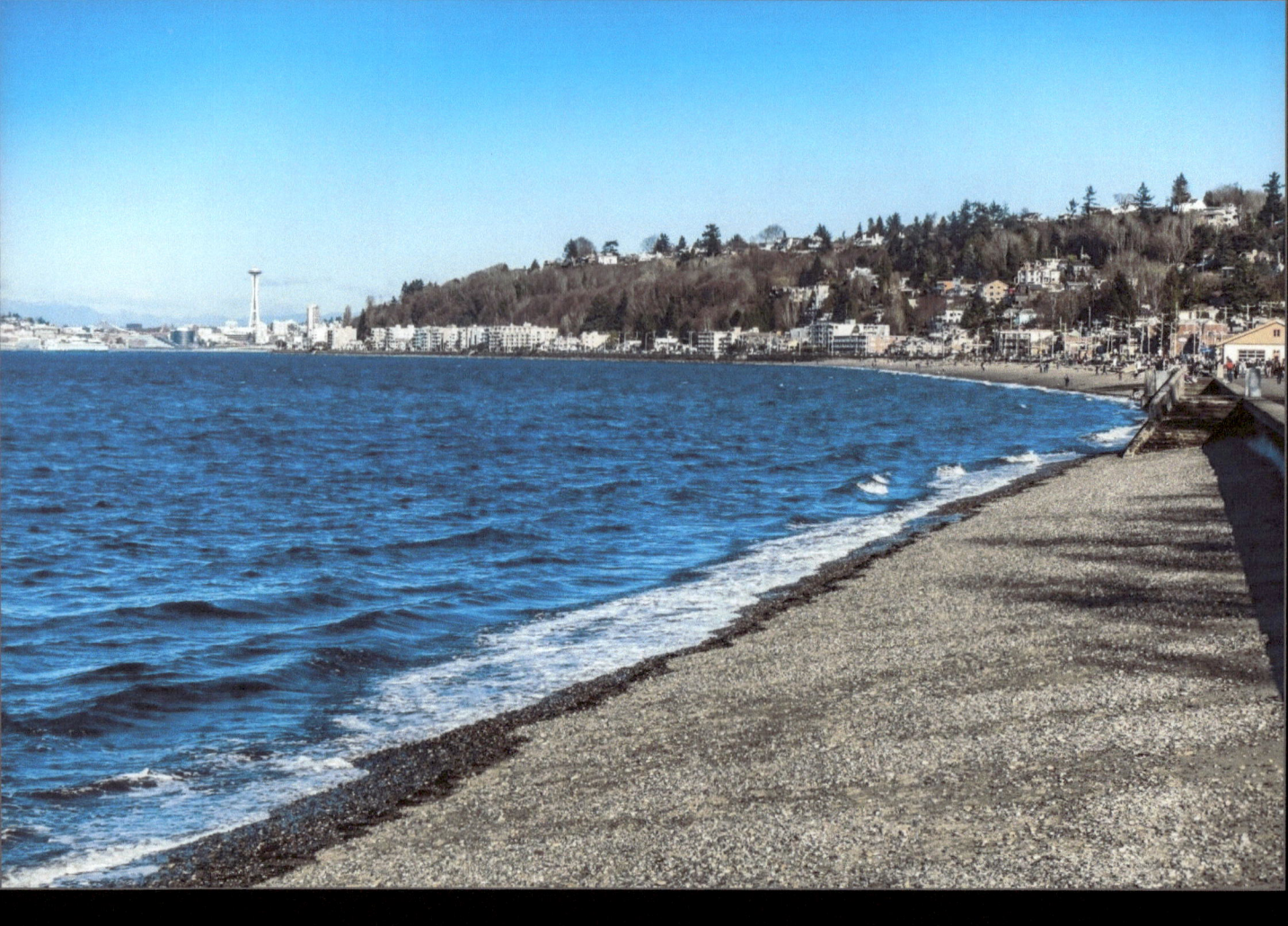

Condominiums line the shore at Alki
Beach in West Seattle, Washington.
Seattle can be seen in the distance.

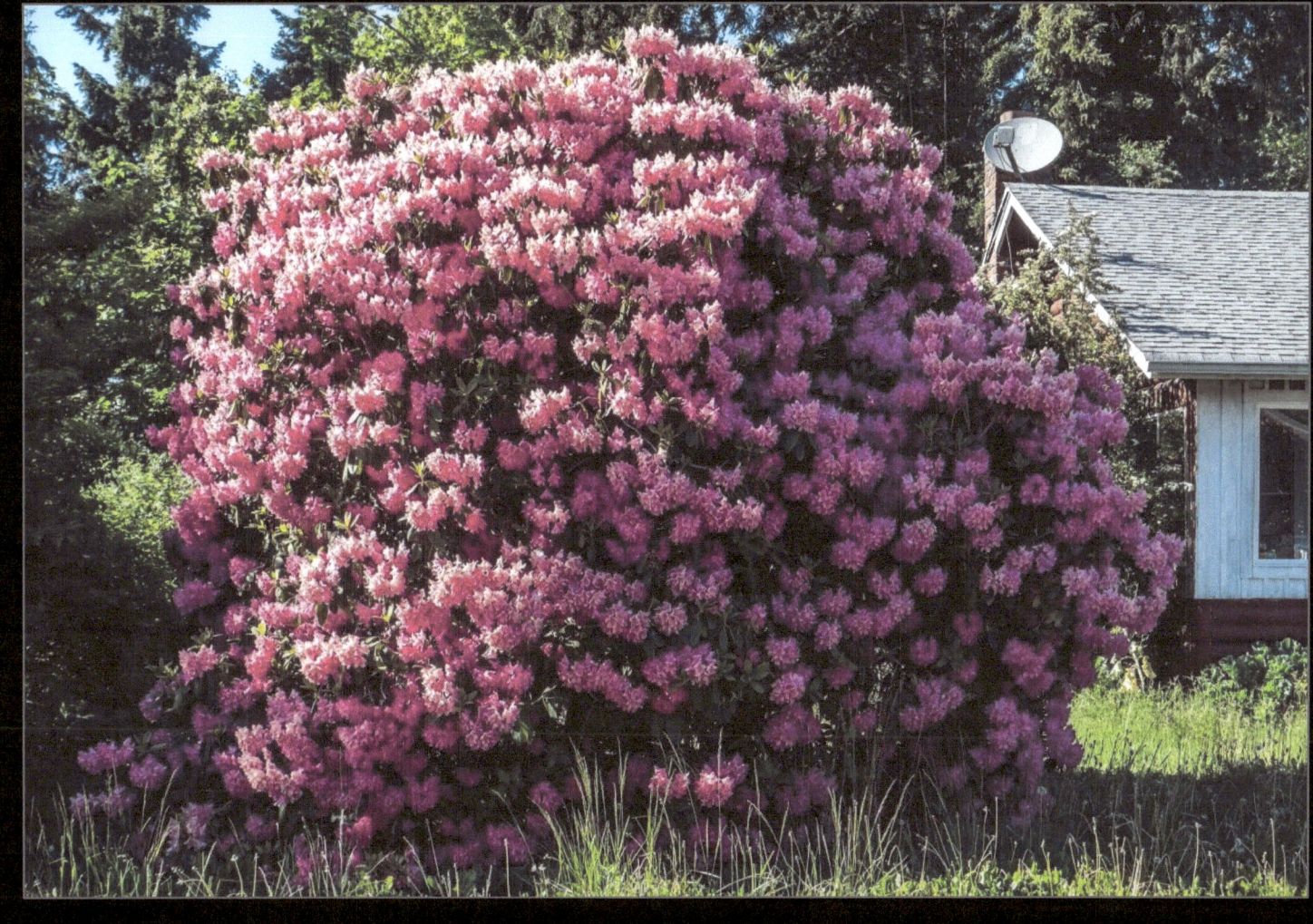

A pink Coast Rhododendron, the
Washington State flower, bursts with
vibrant color.

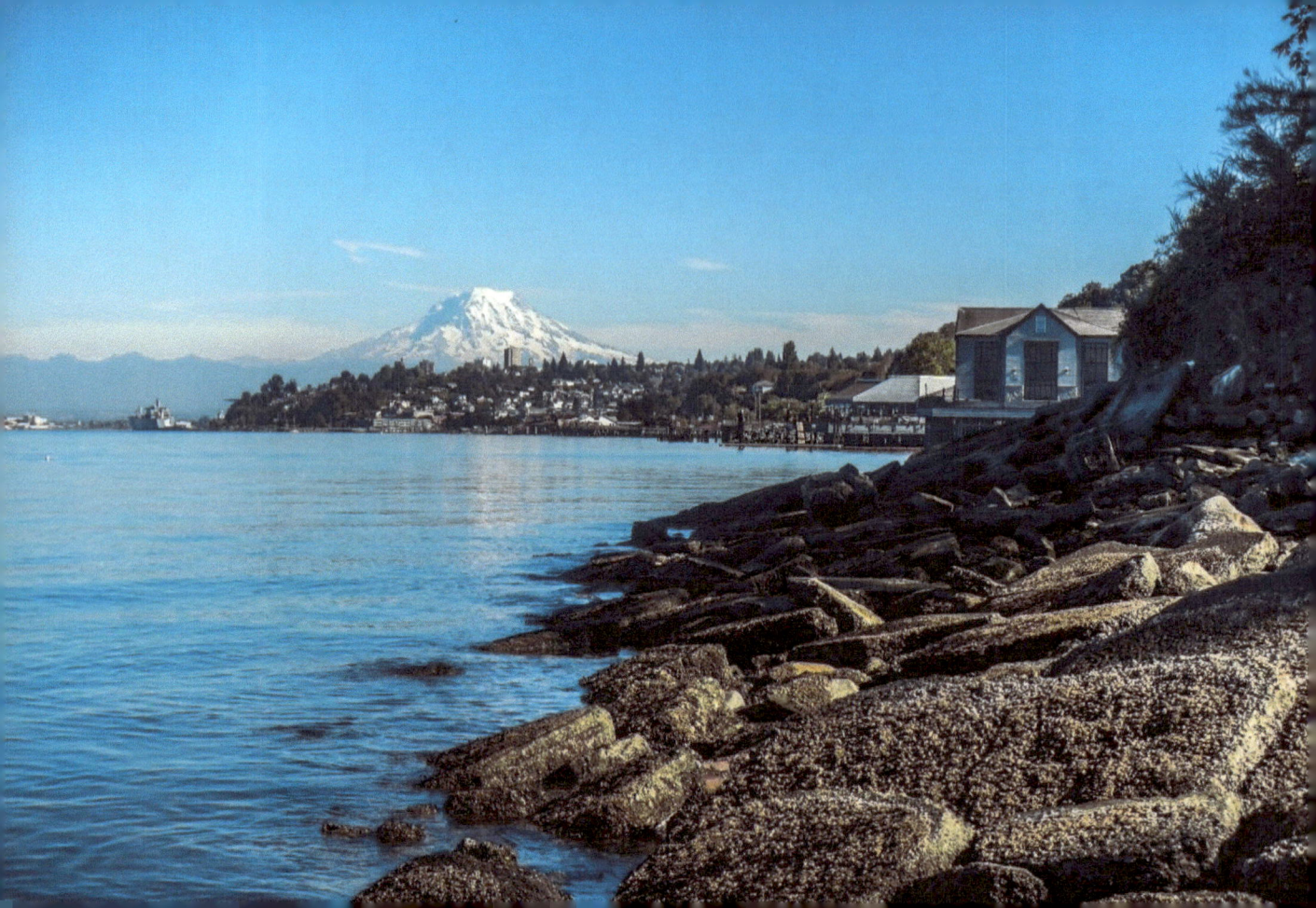

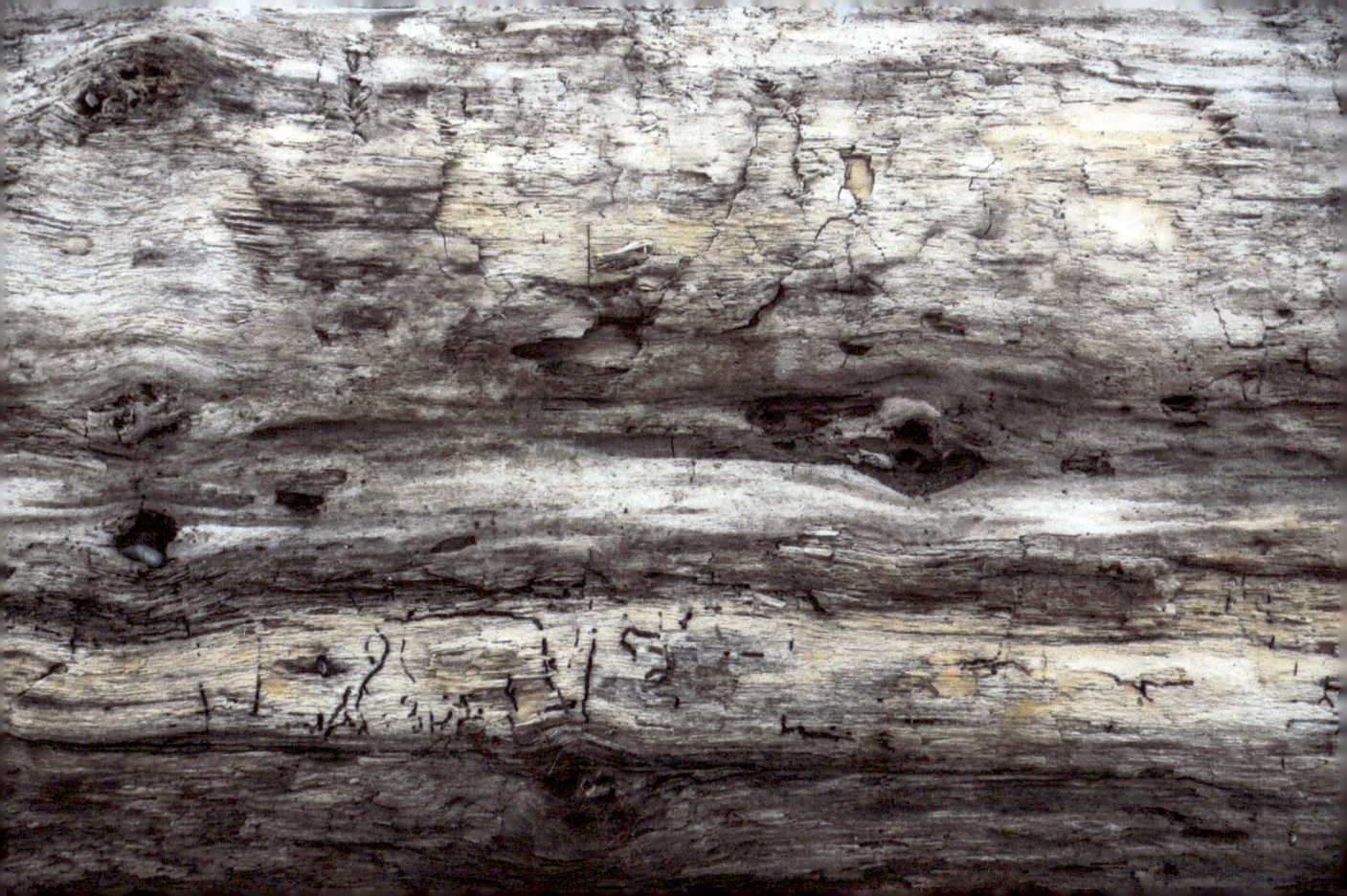

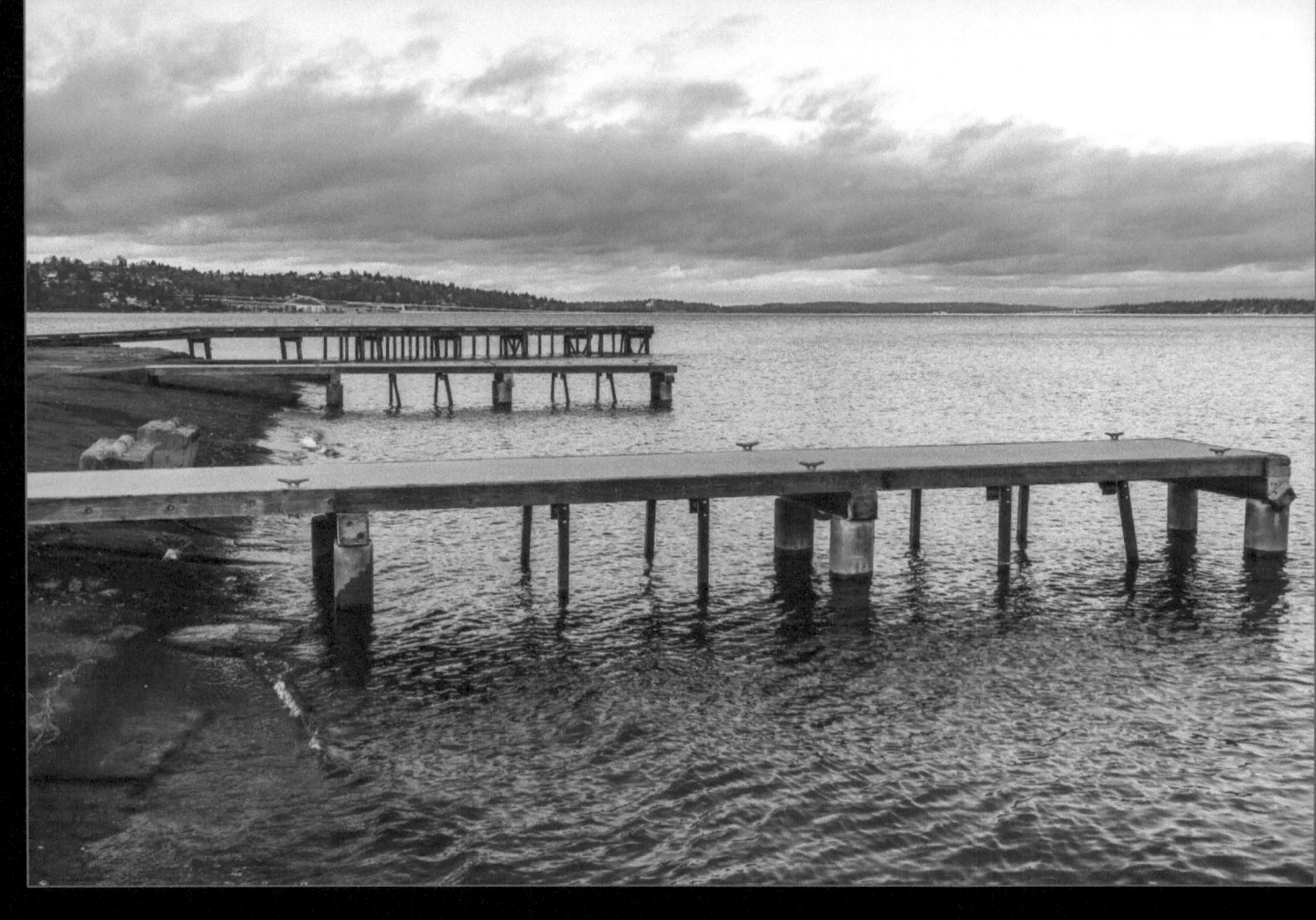

Piers jut out on to Lake Washington
near Seattle late in the day.

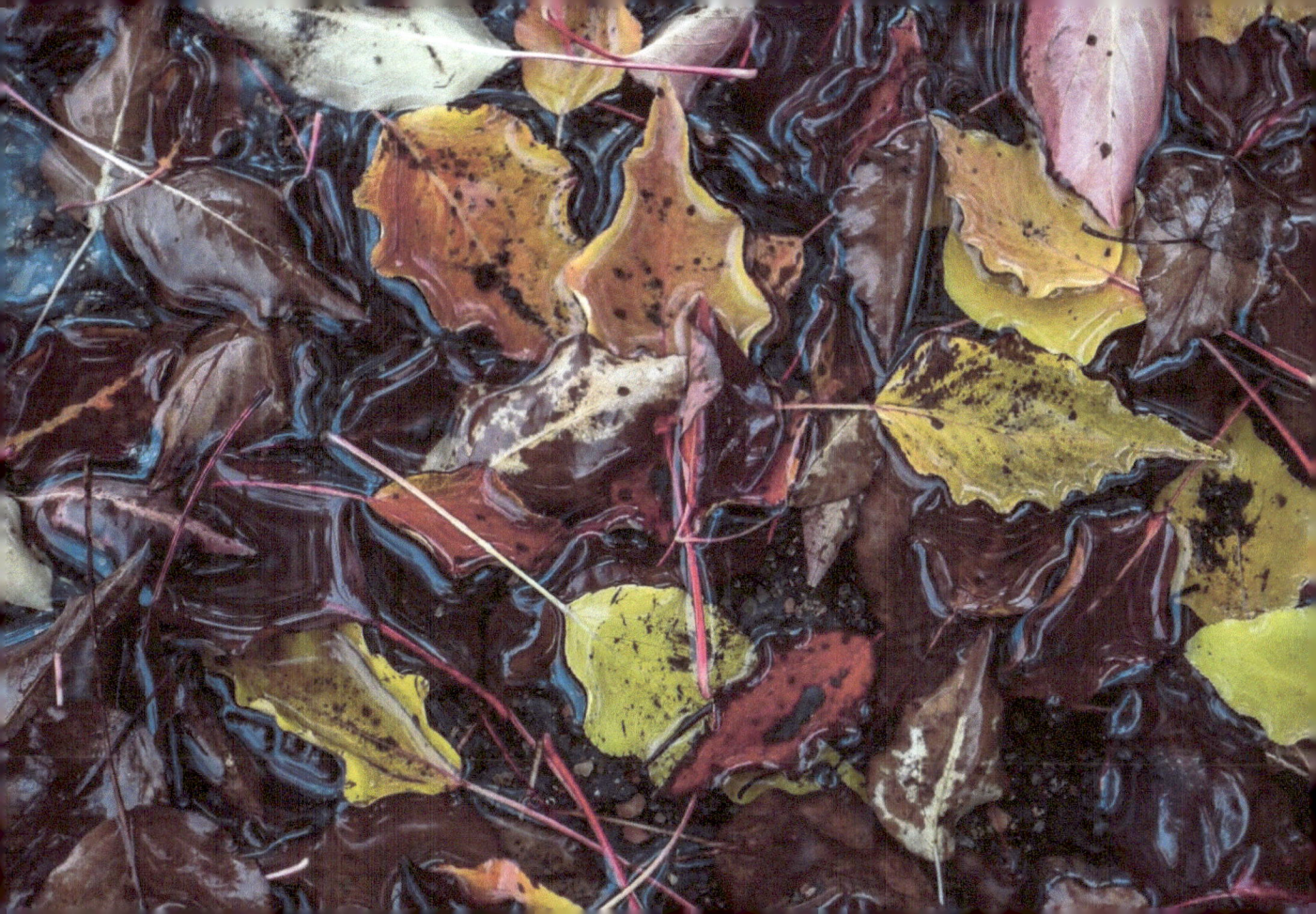

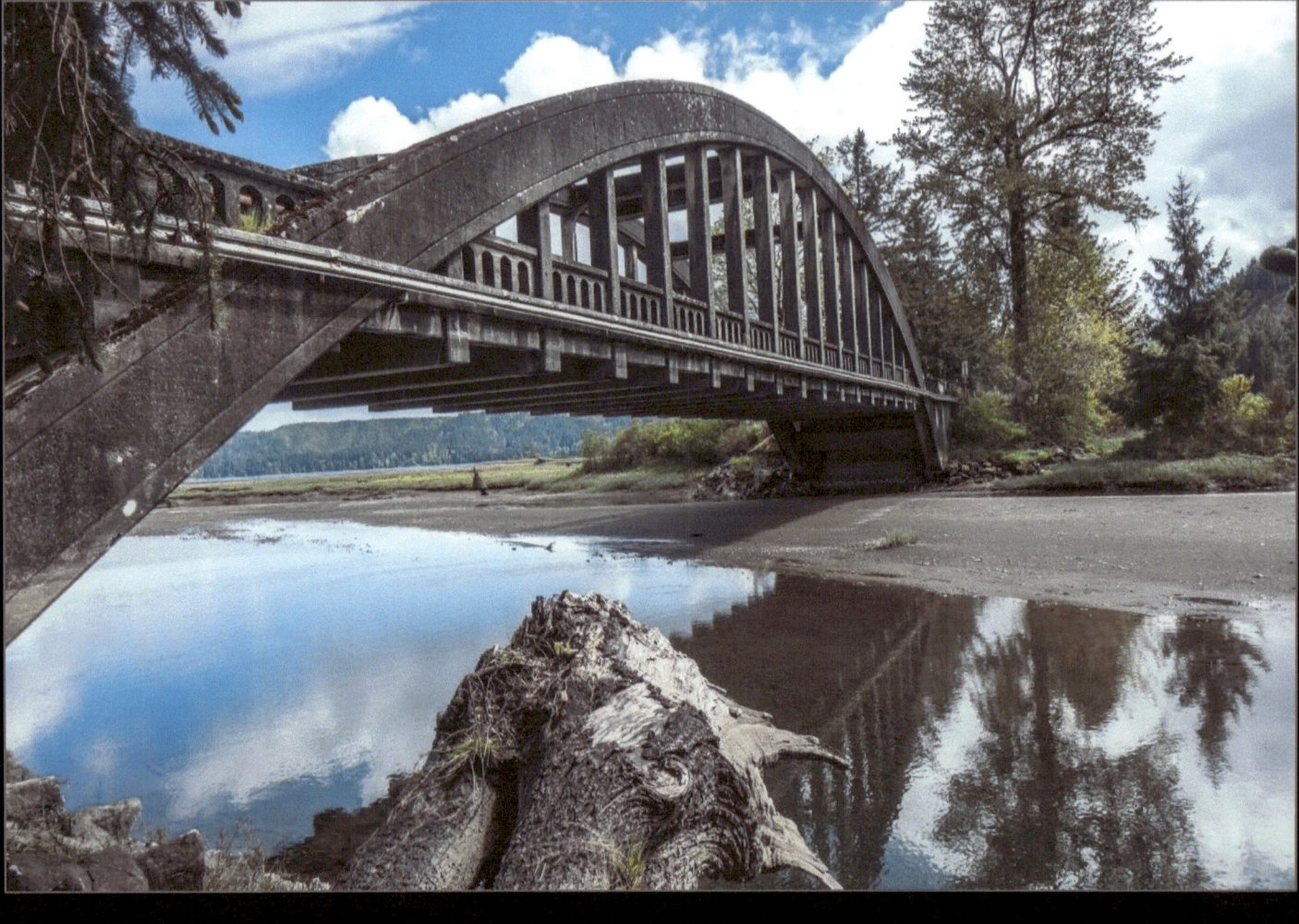

An old but stately bridge spans a river that flows into the Hood Canal in Washington State.

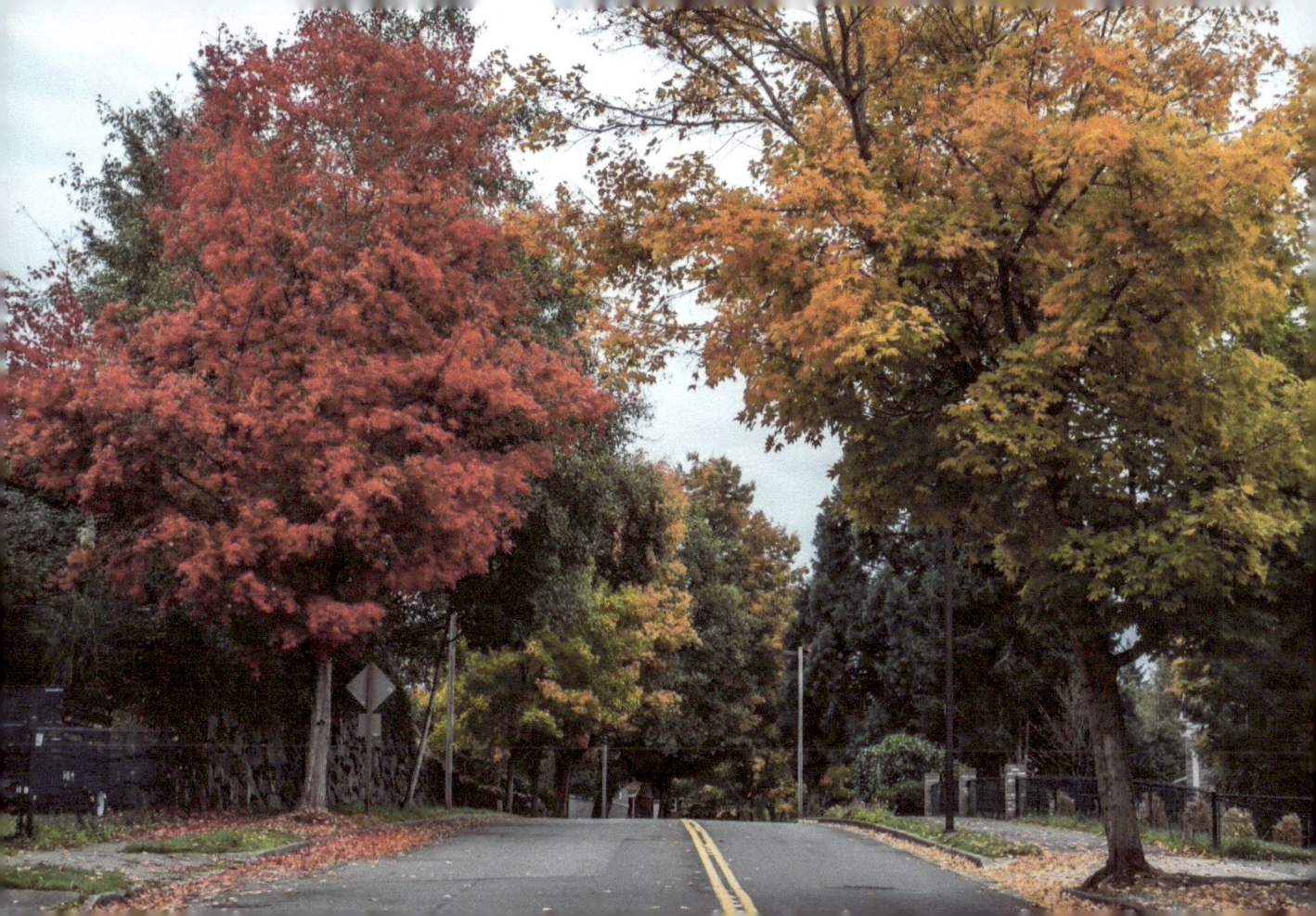

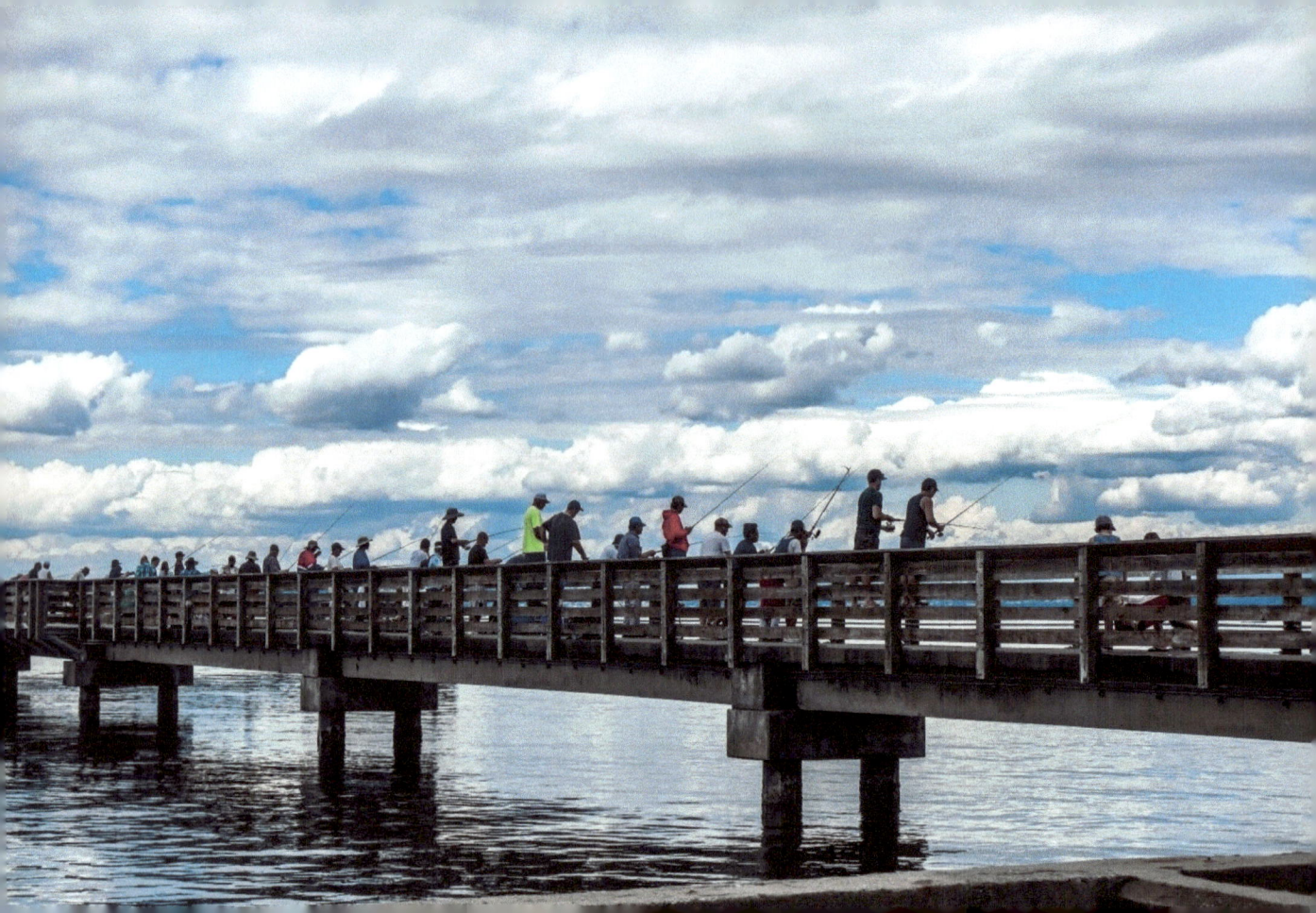

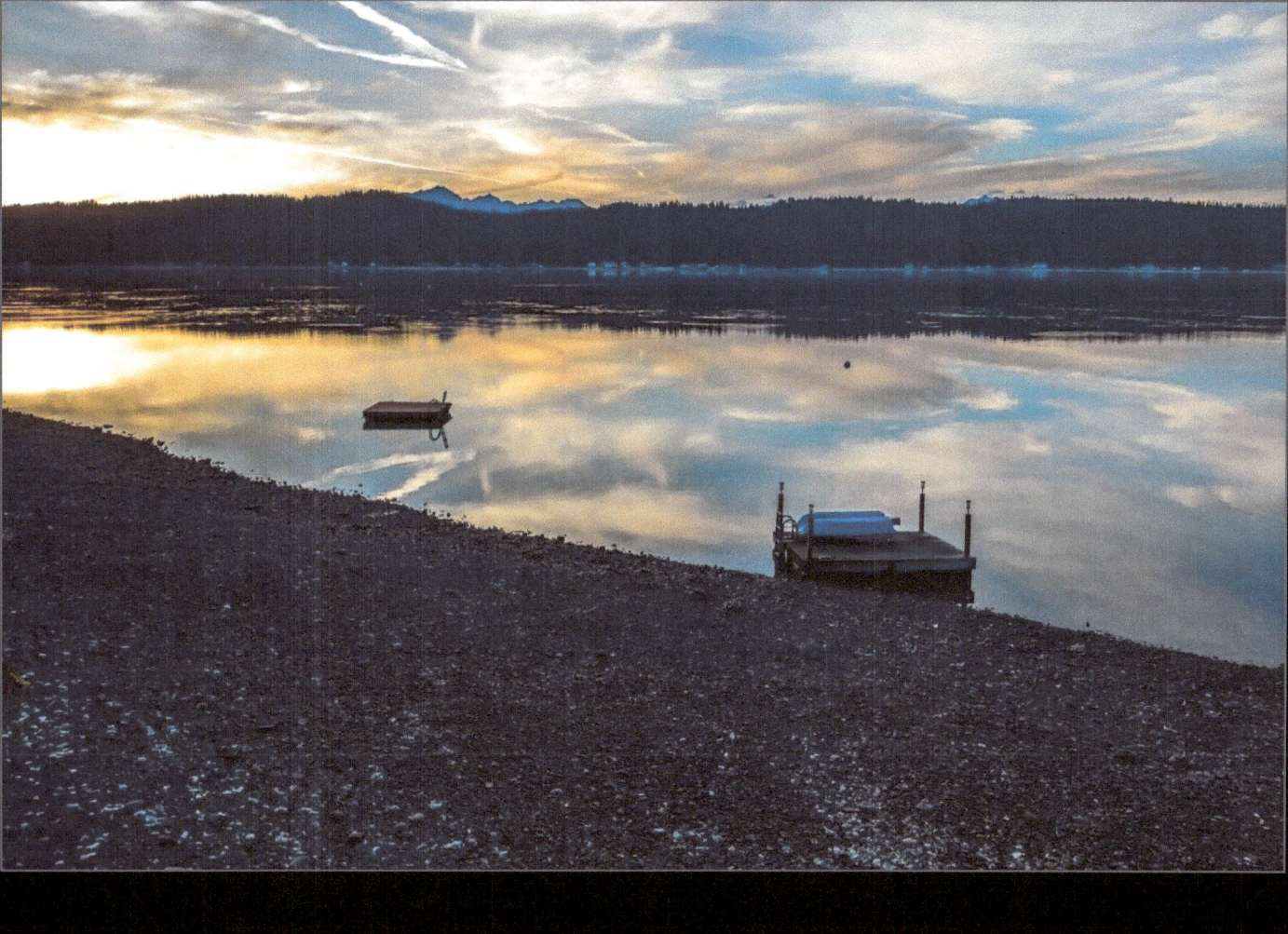

The sunset behind the Olympic Mountains

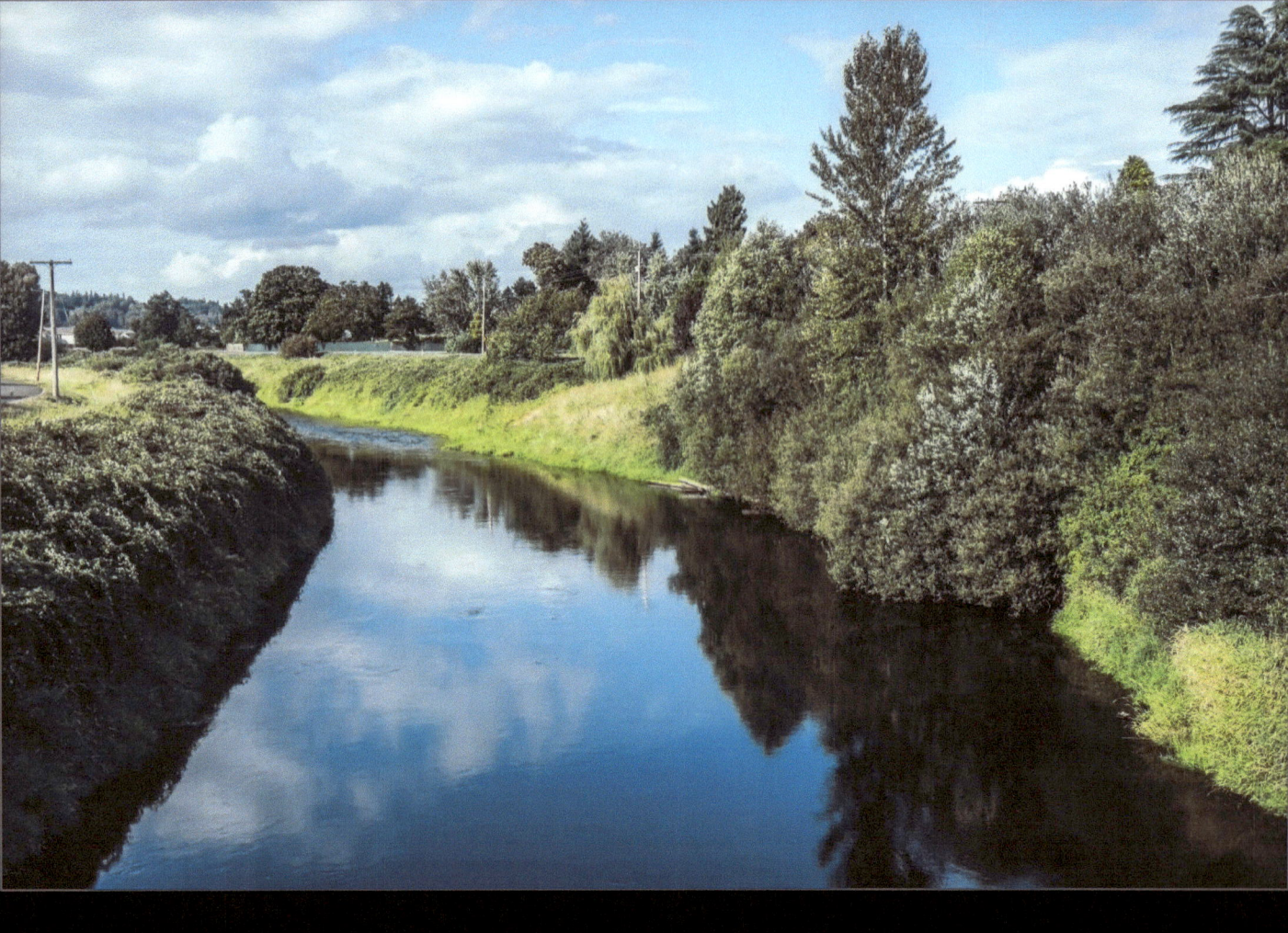

Delicate clouds are reflected in the

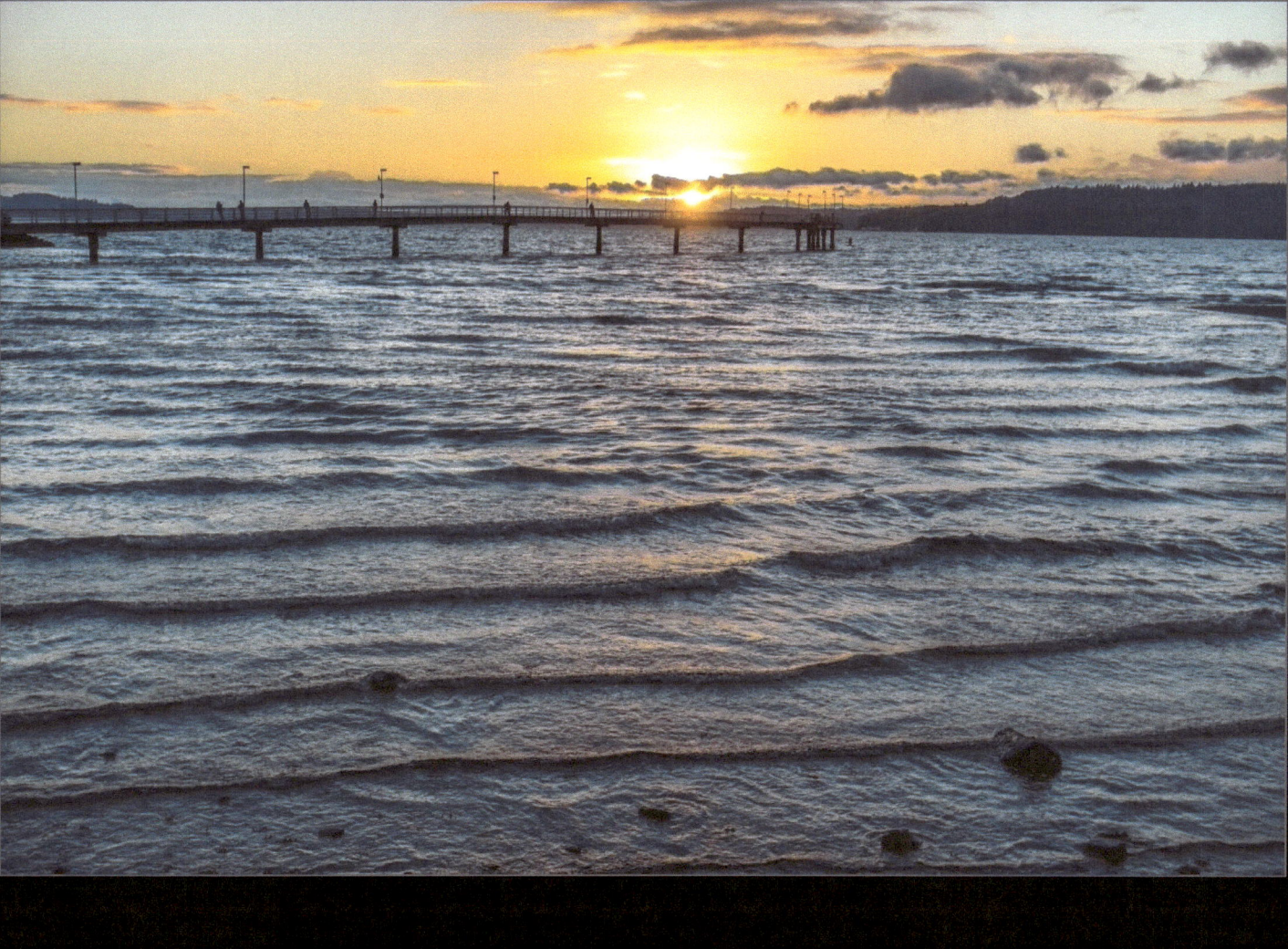

Waves from the Puget Sound roll toward shore as the sun sets behind the pier in Des Moines, Washington.

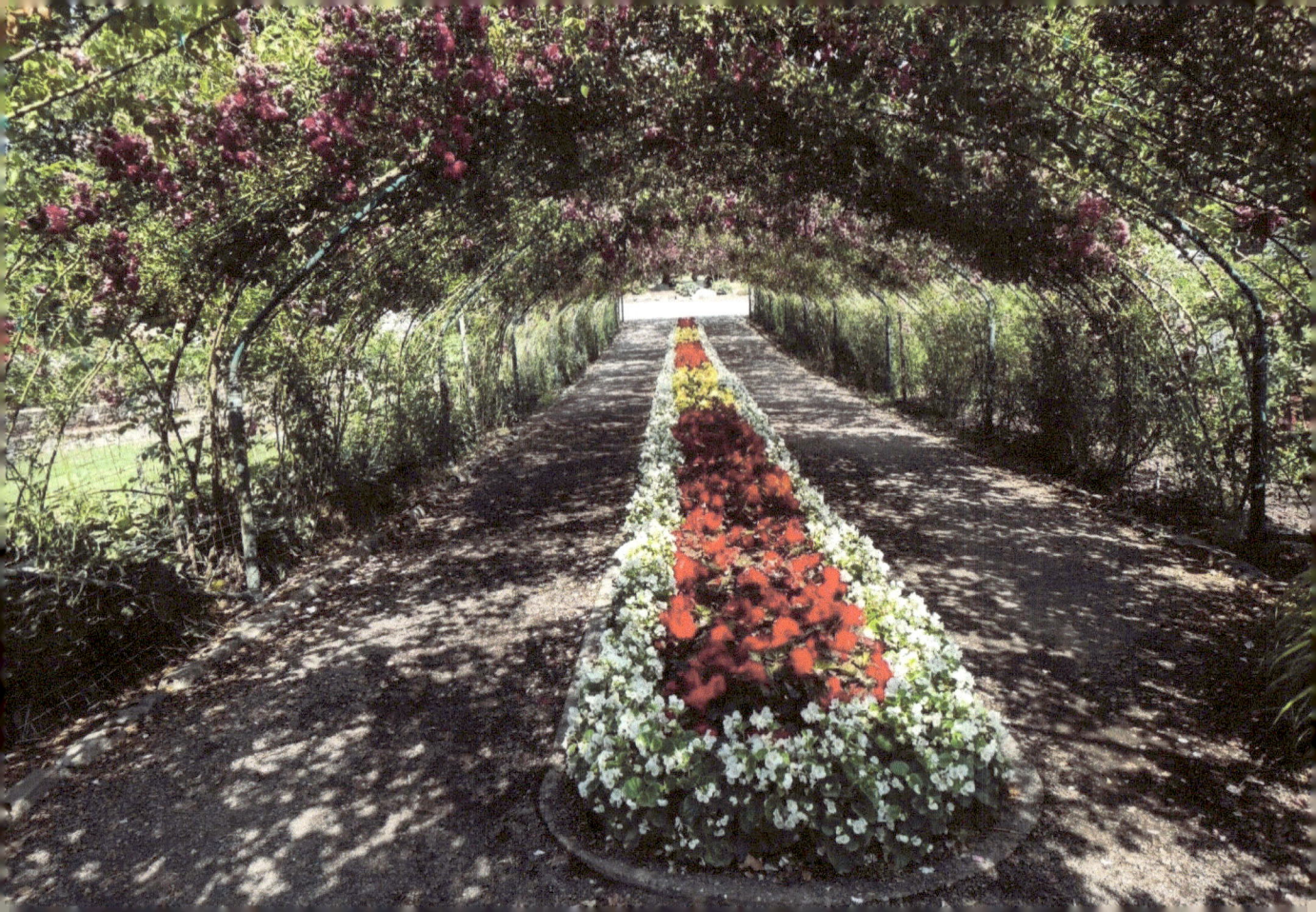

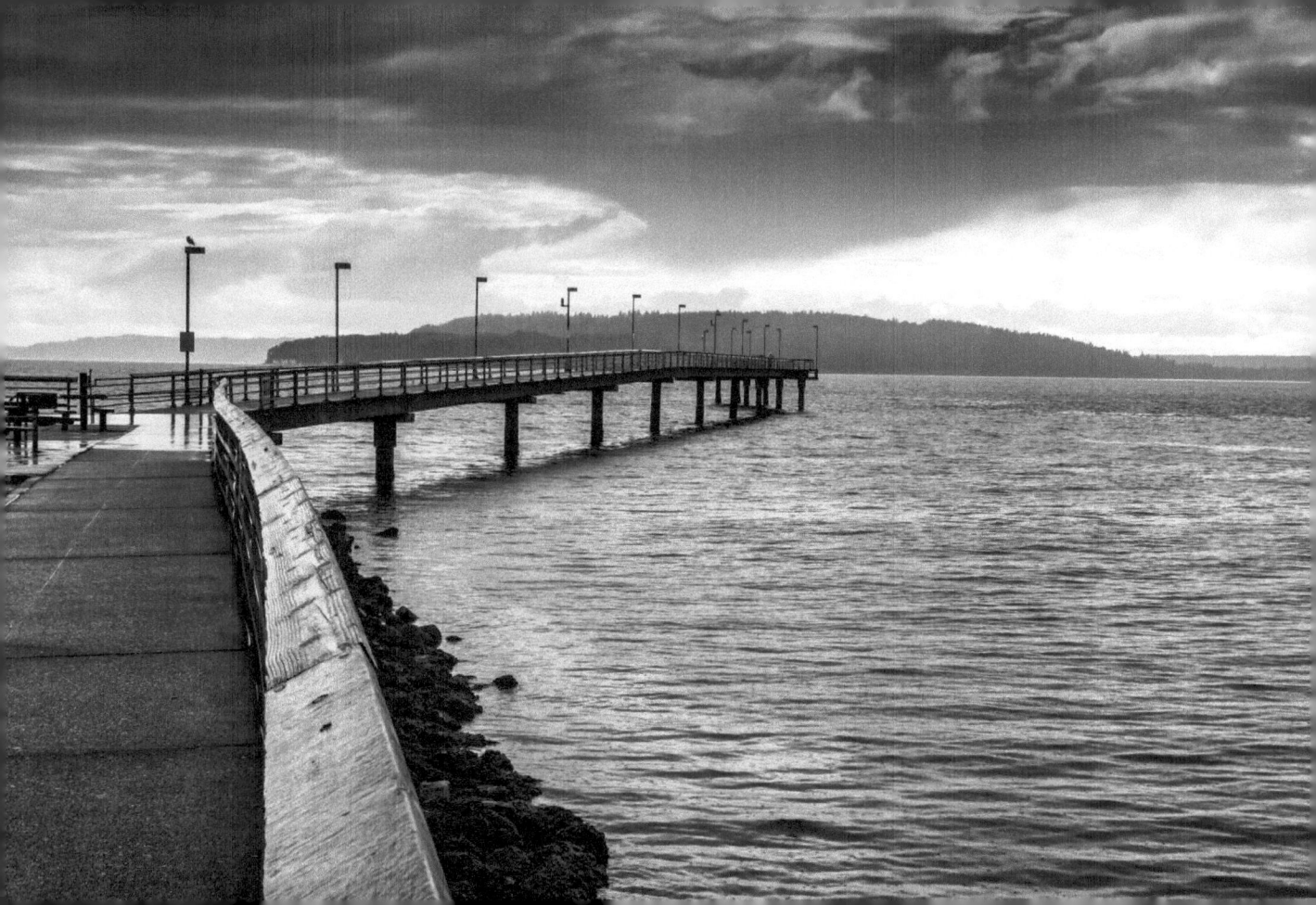

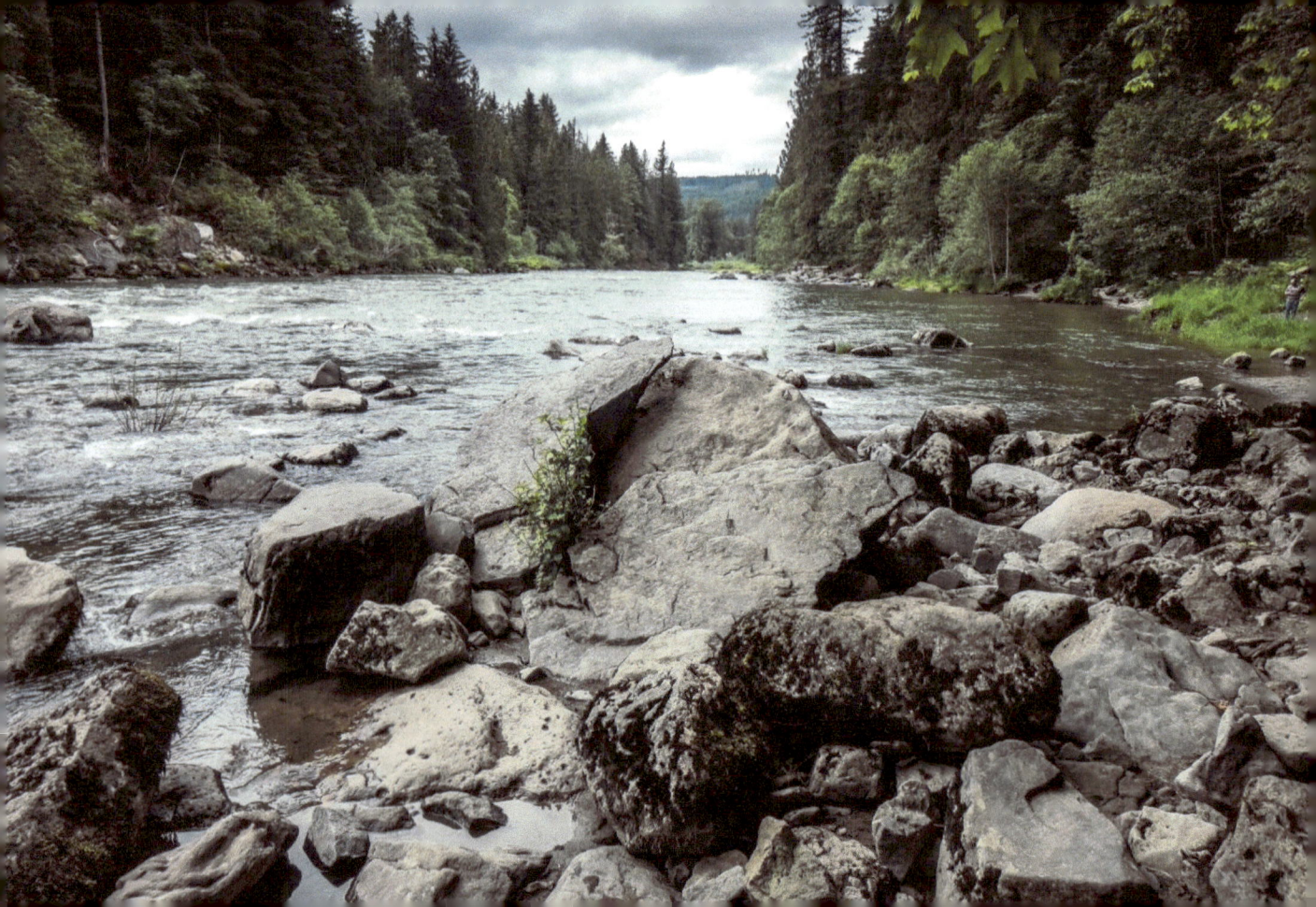

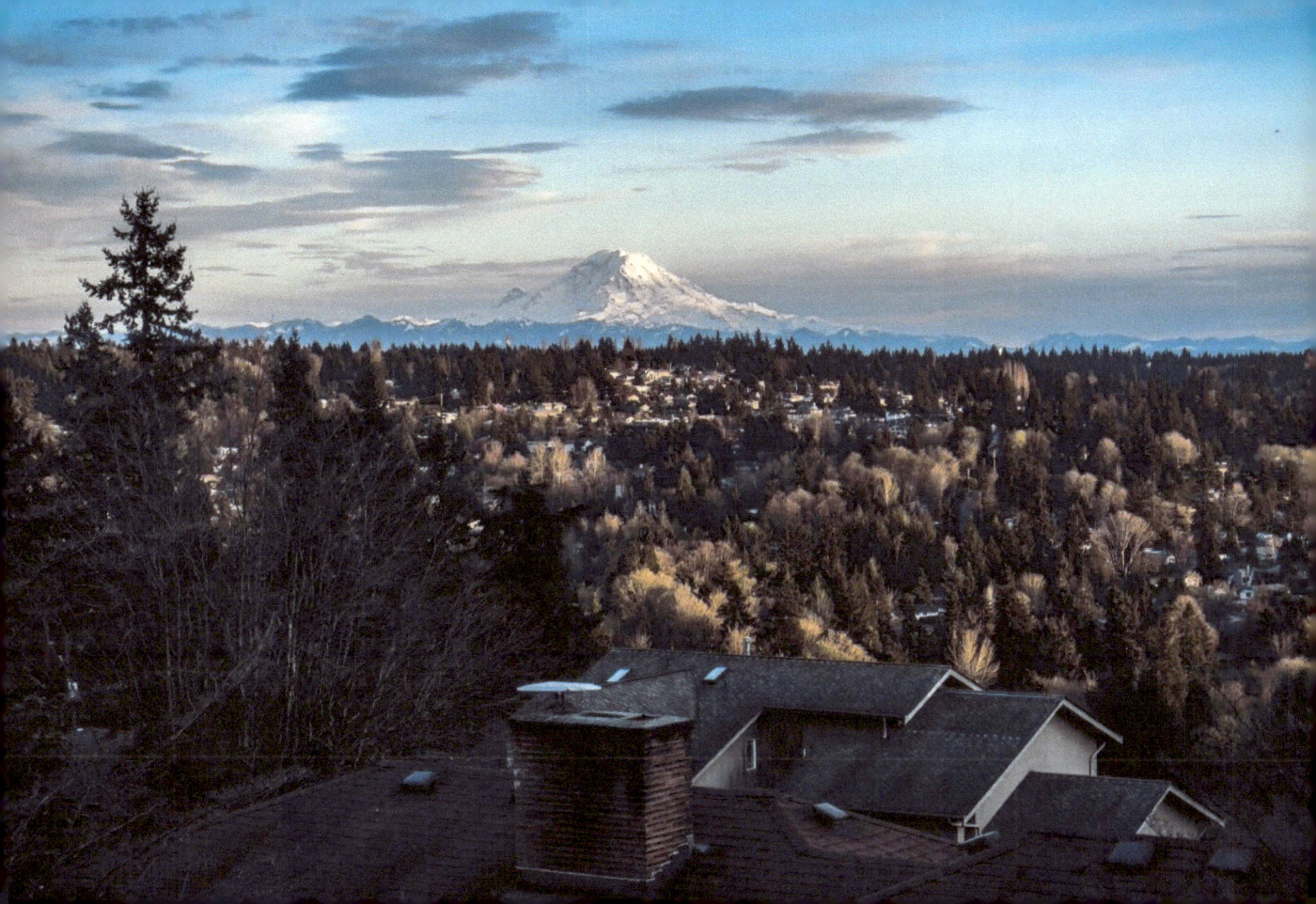

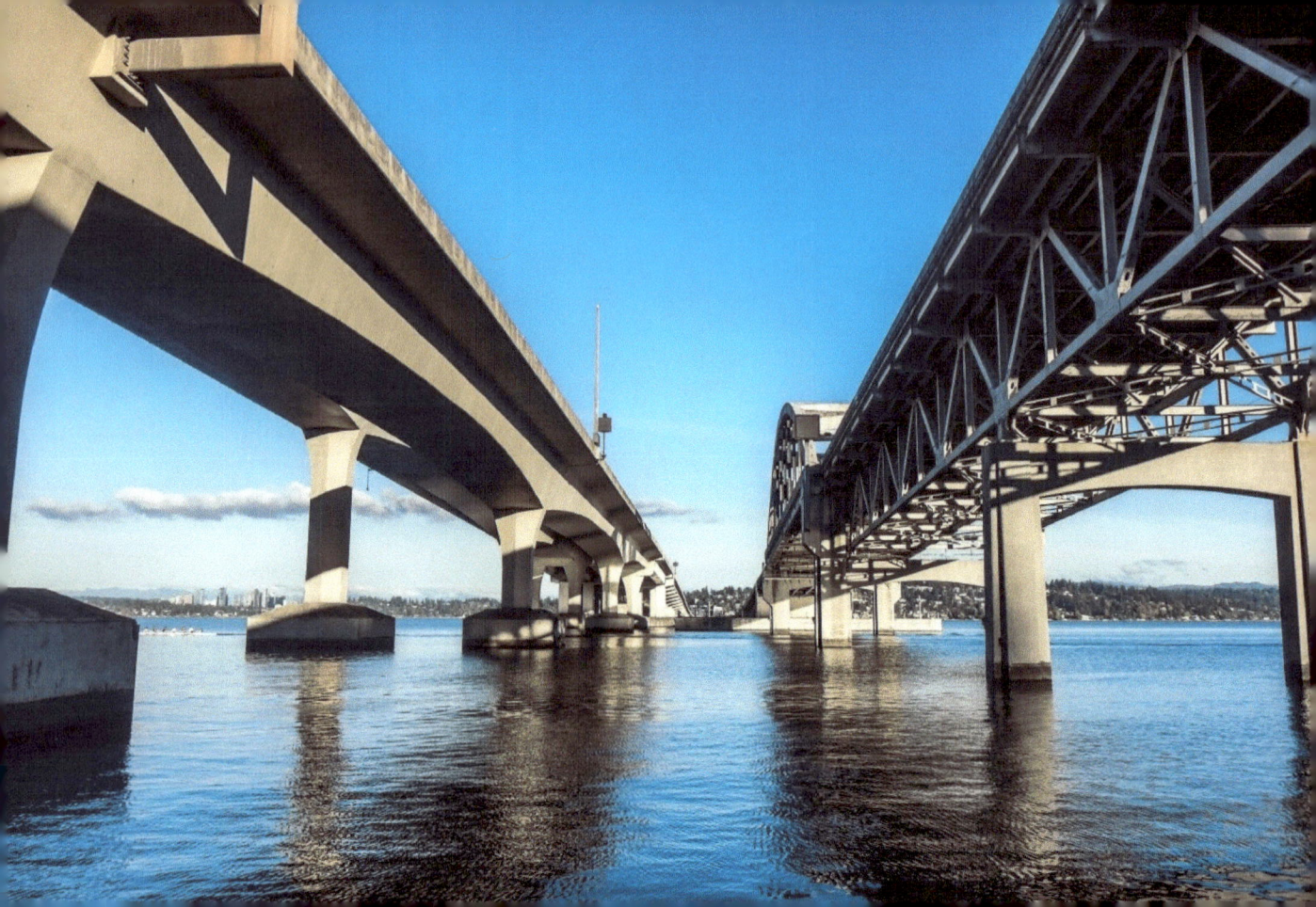

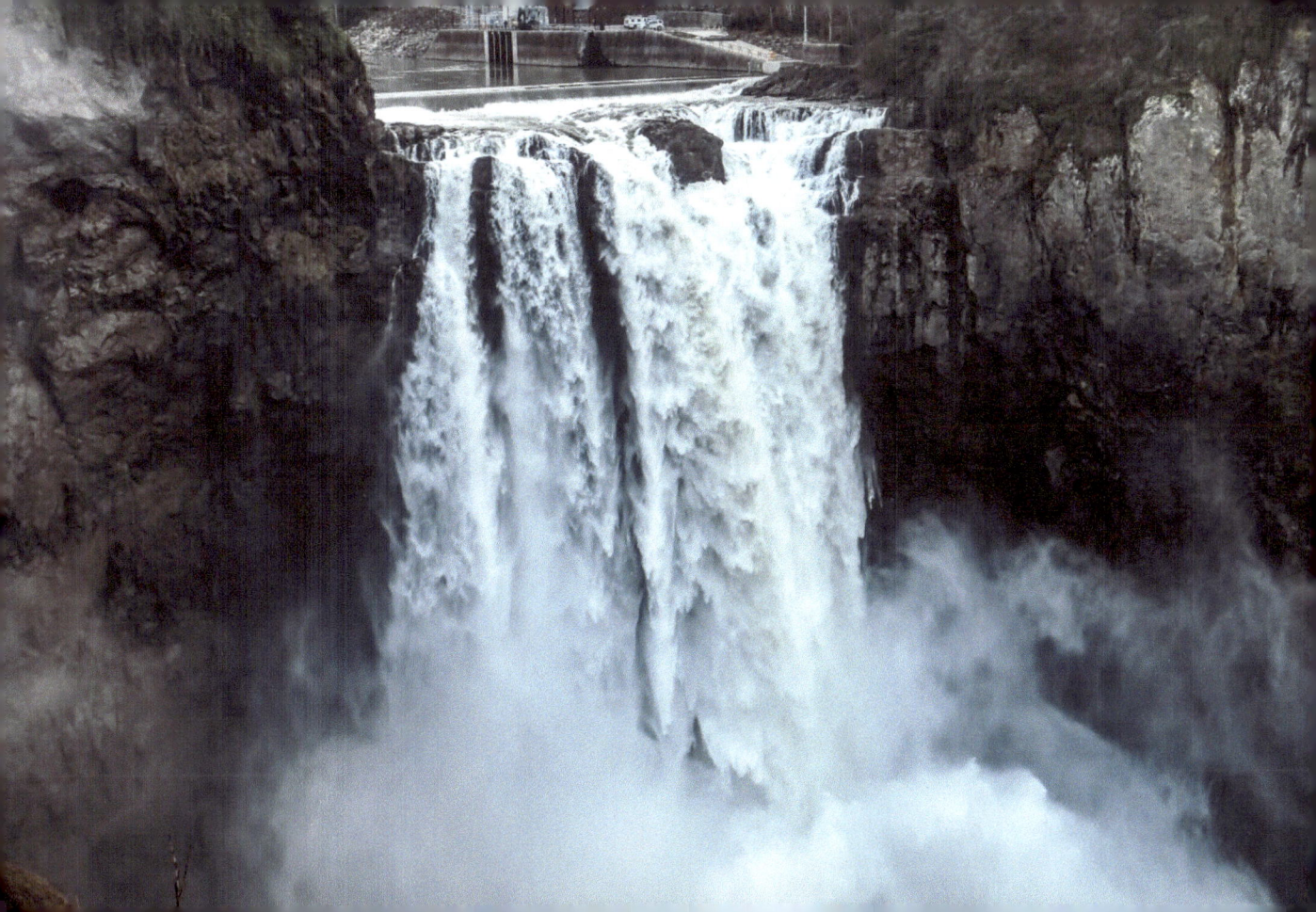

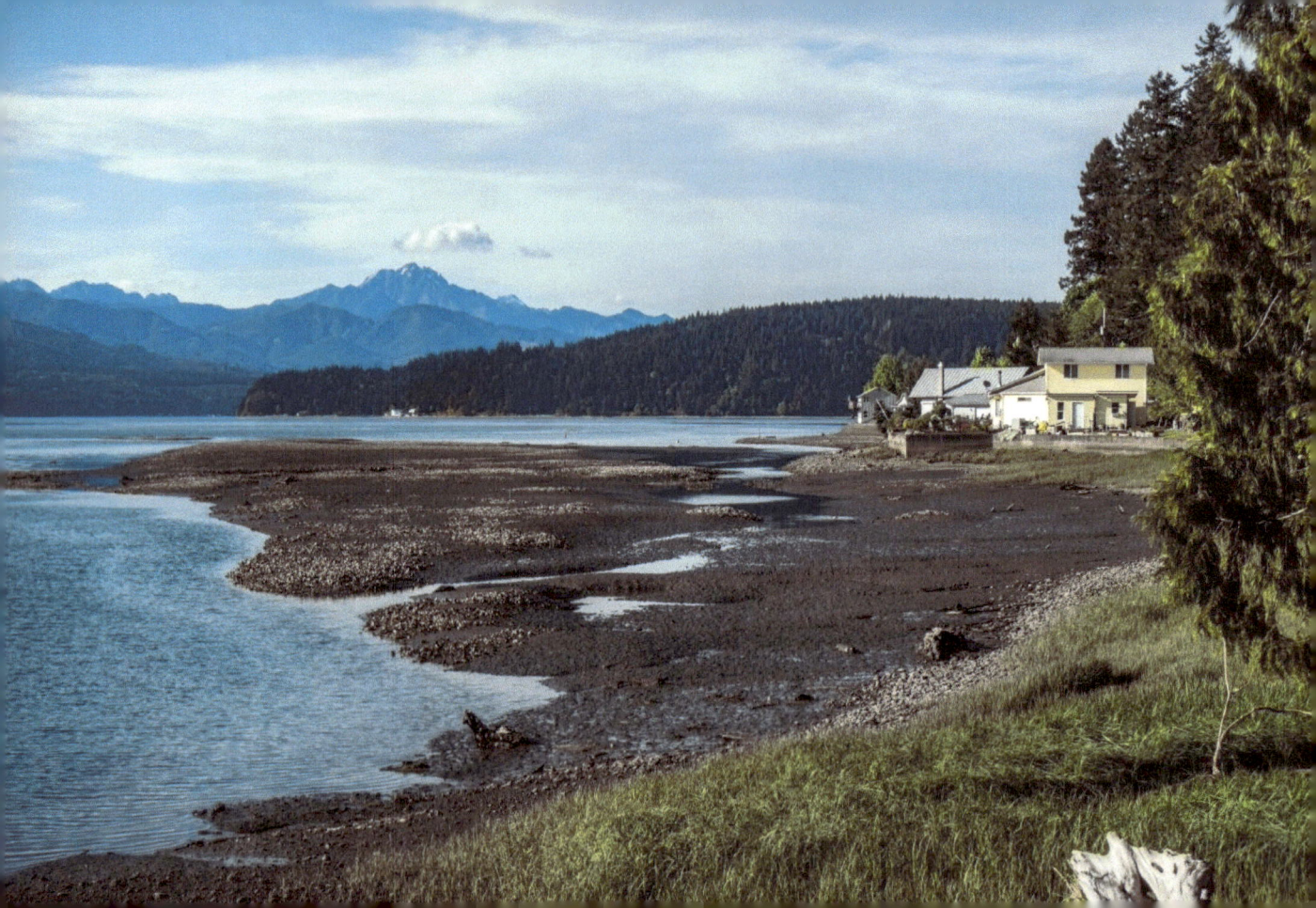

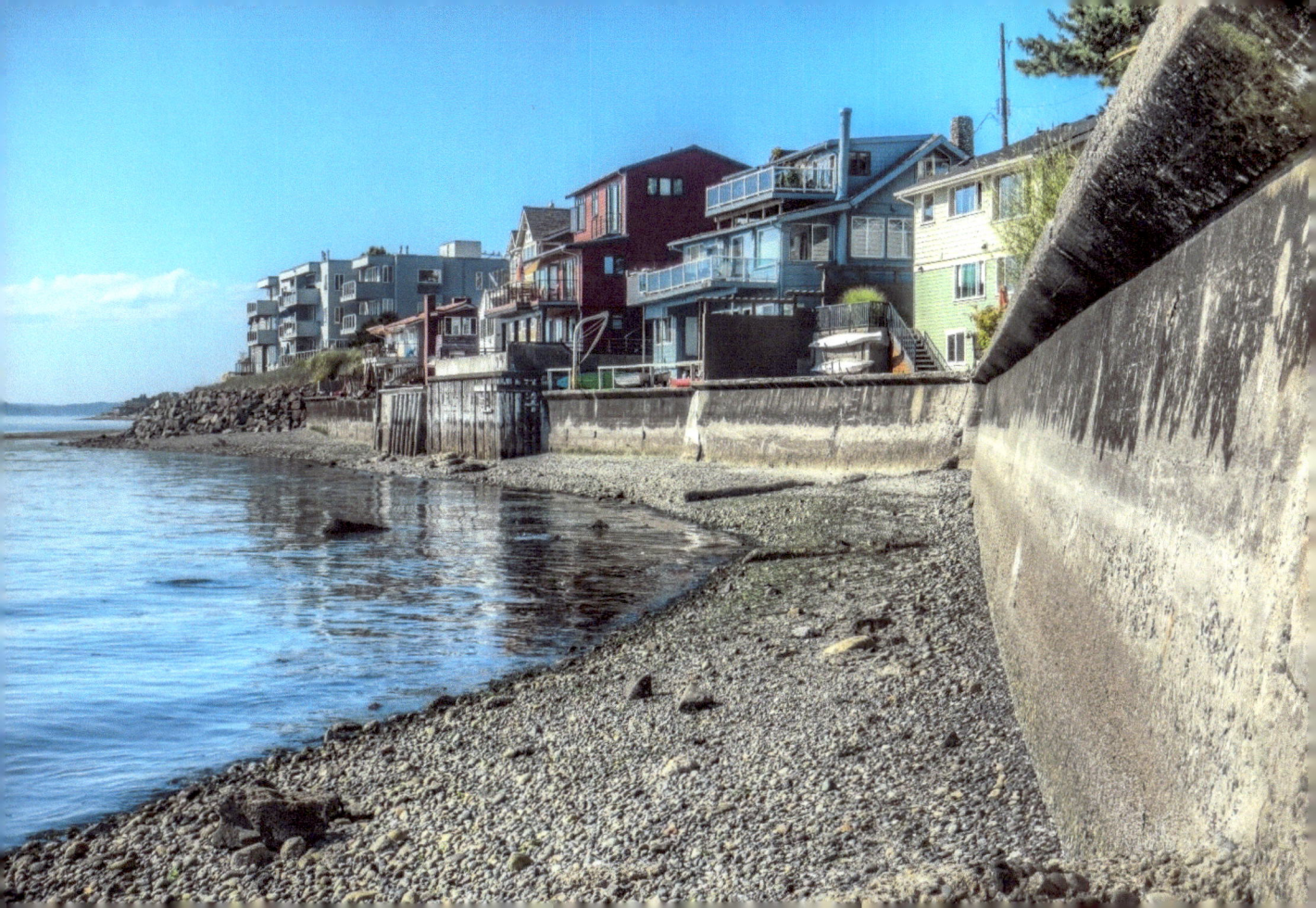

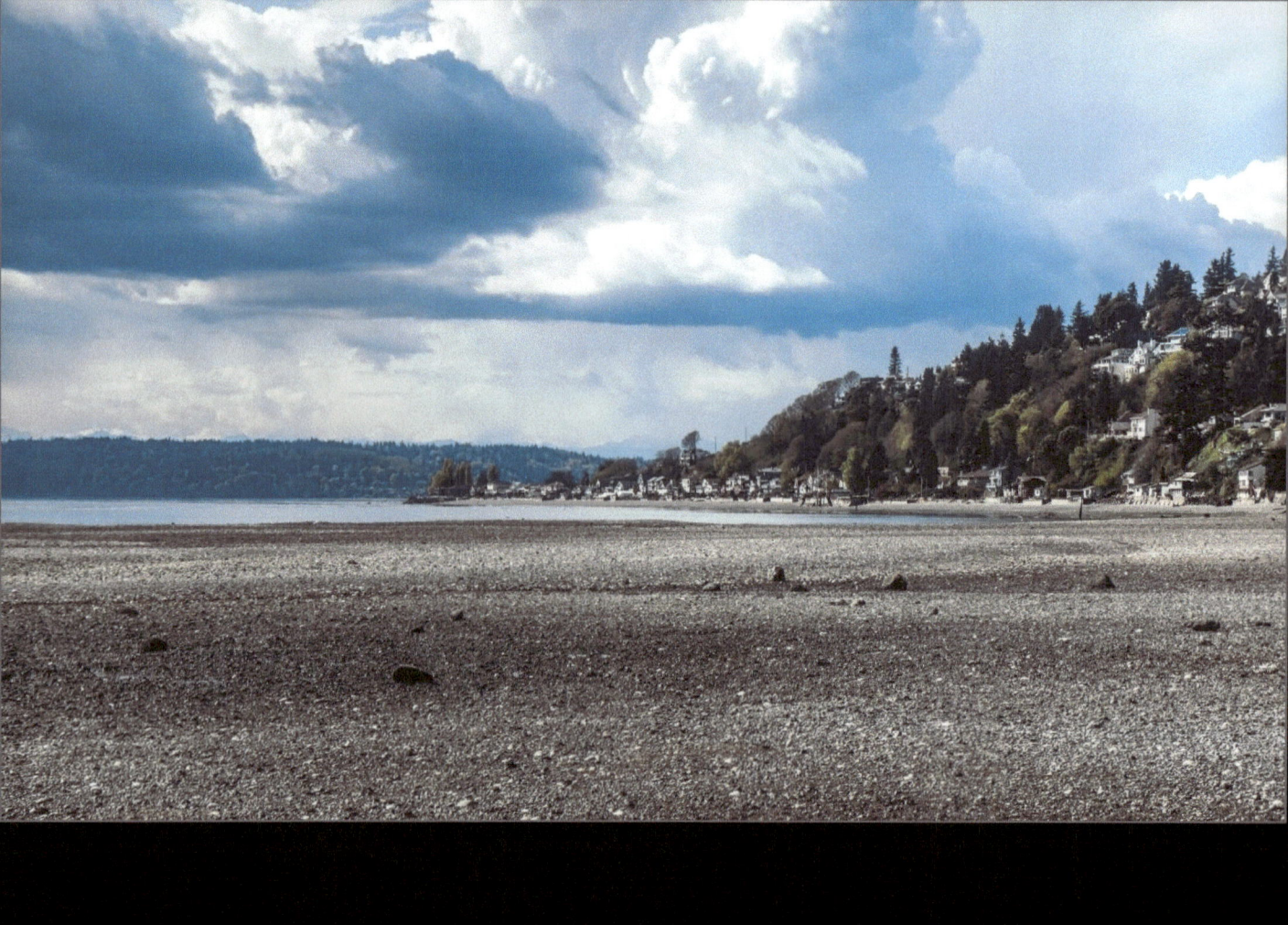

The tide is low on a cloudy day at Three Tree
Point in Burien, Washington.

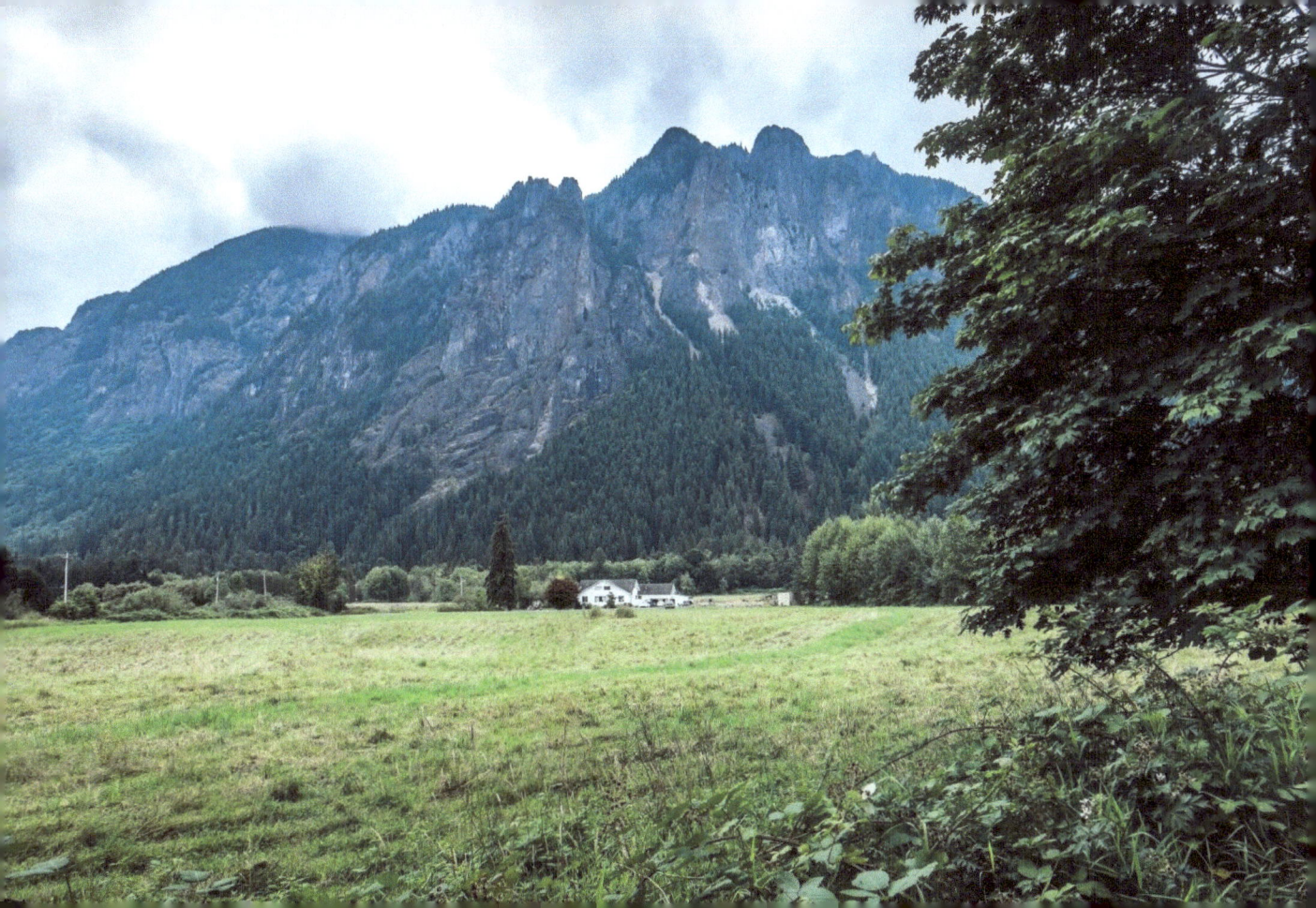

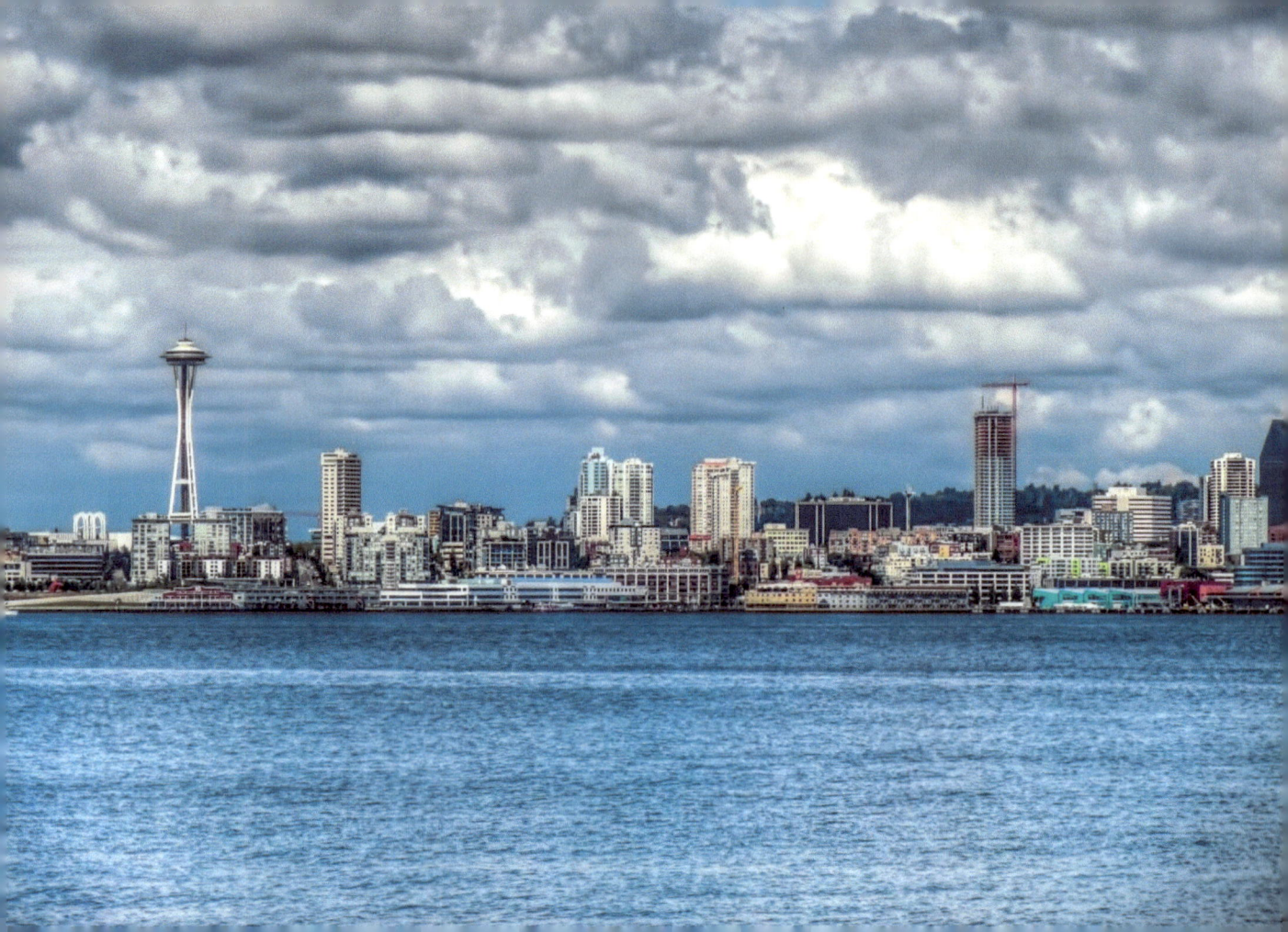

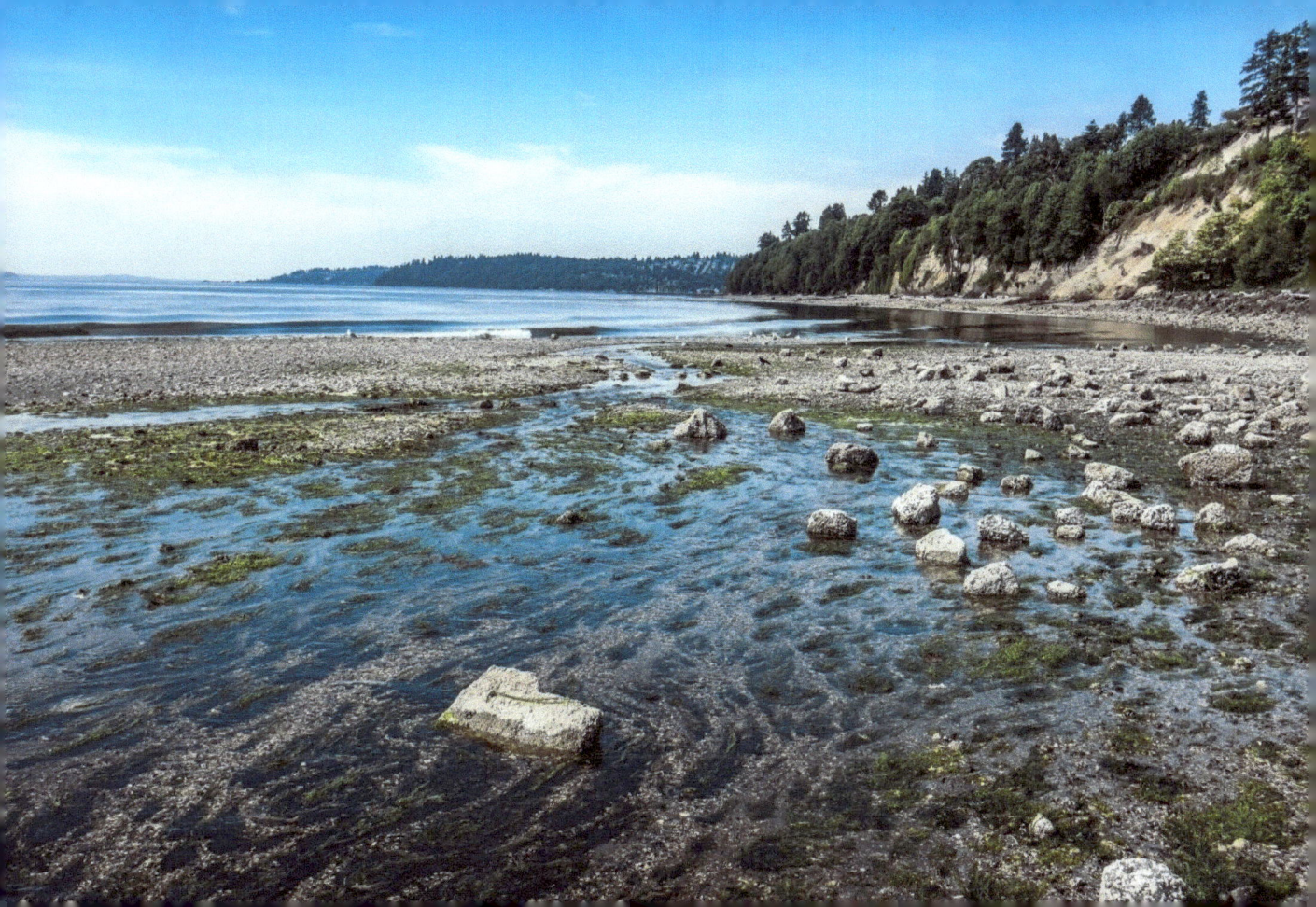

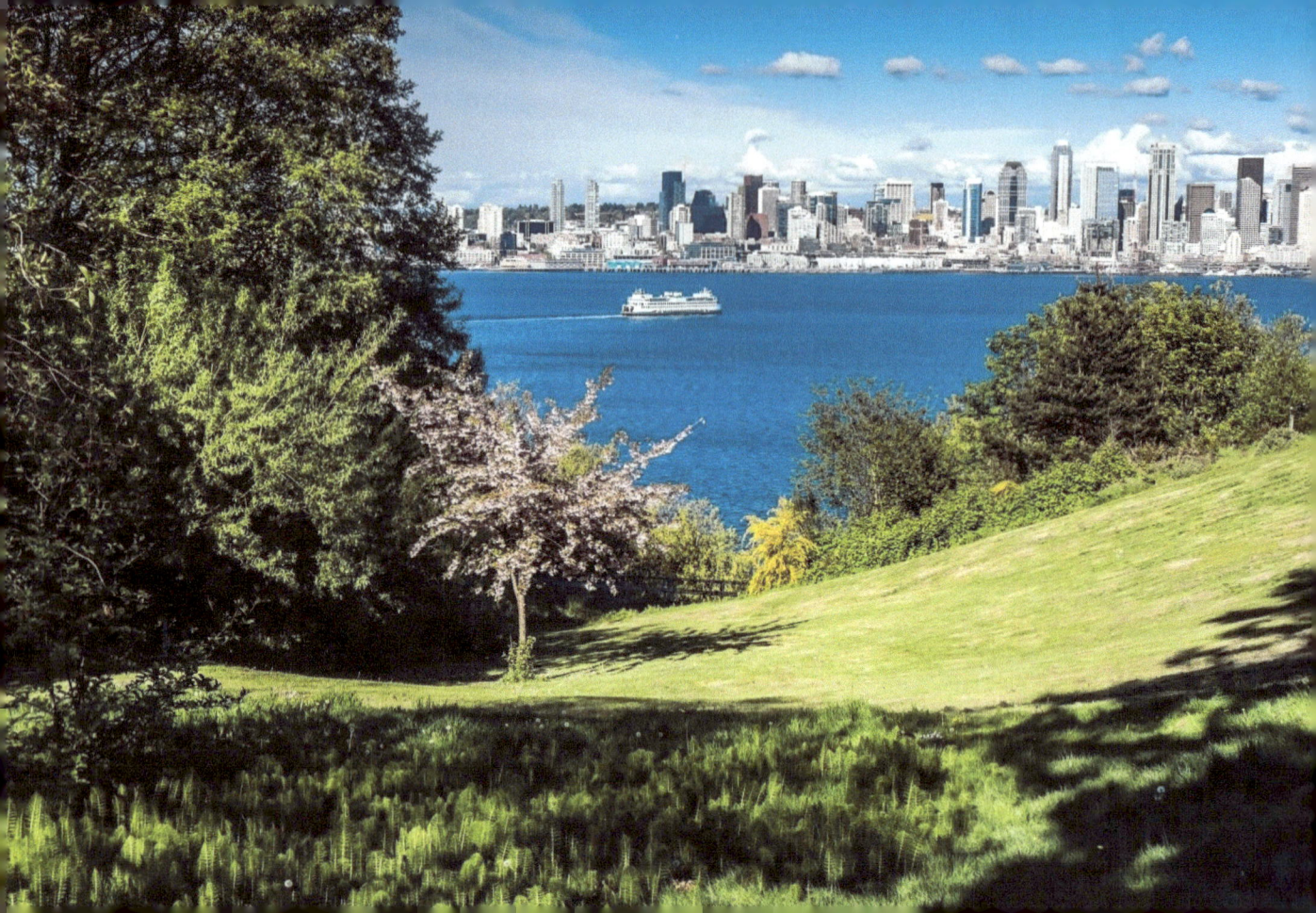

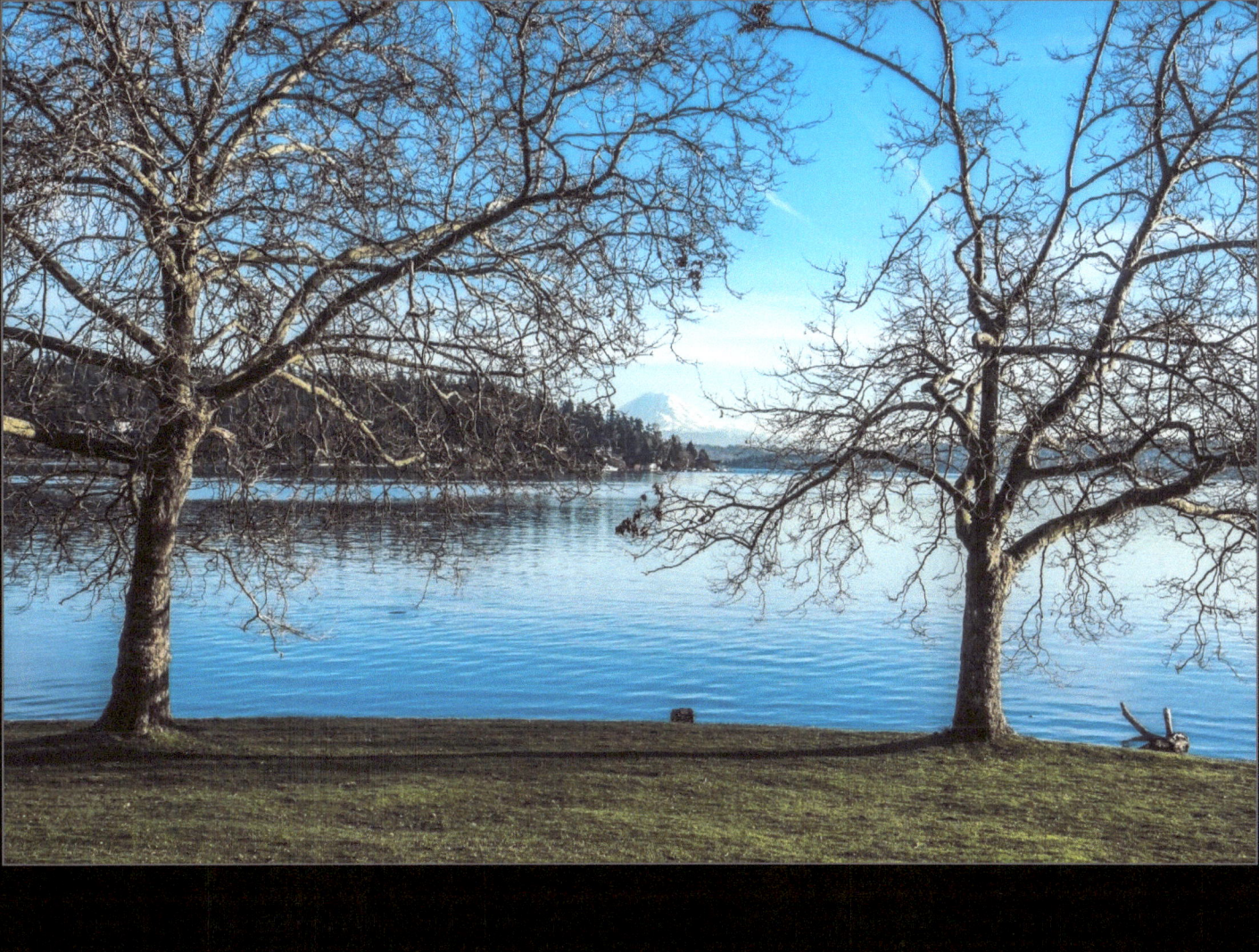

Mount Rainier across Lake Washington is
framed by two trees in Spring. Photo taken
from Seward Park in Seattle, Washington.

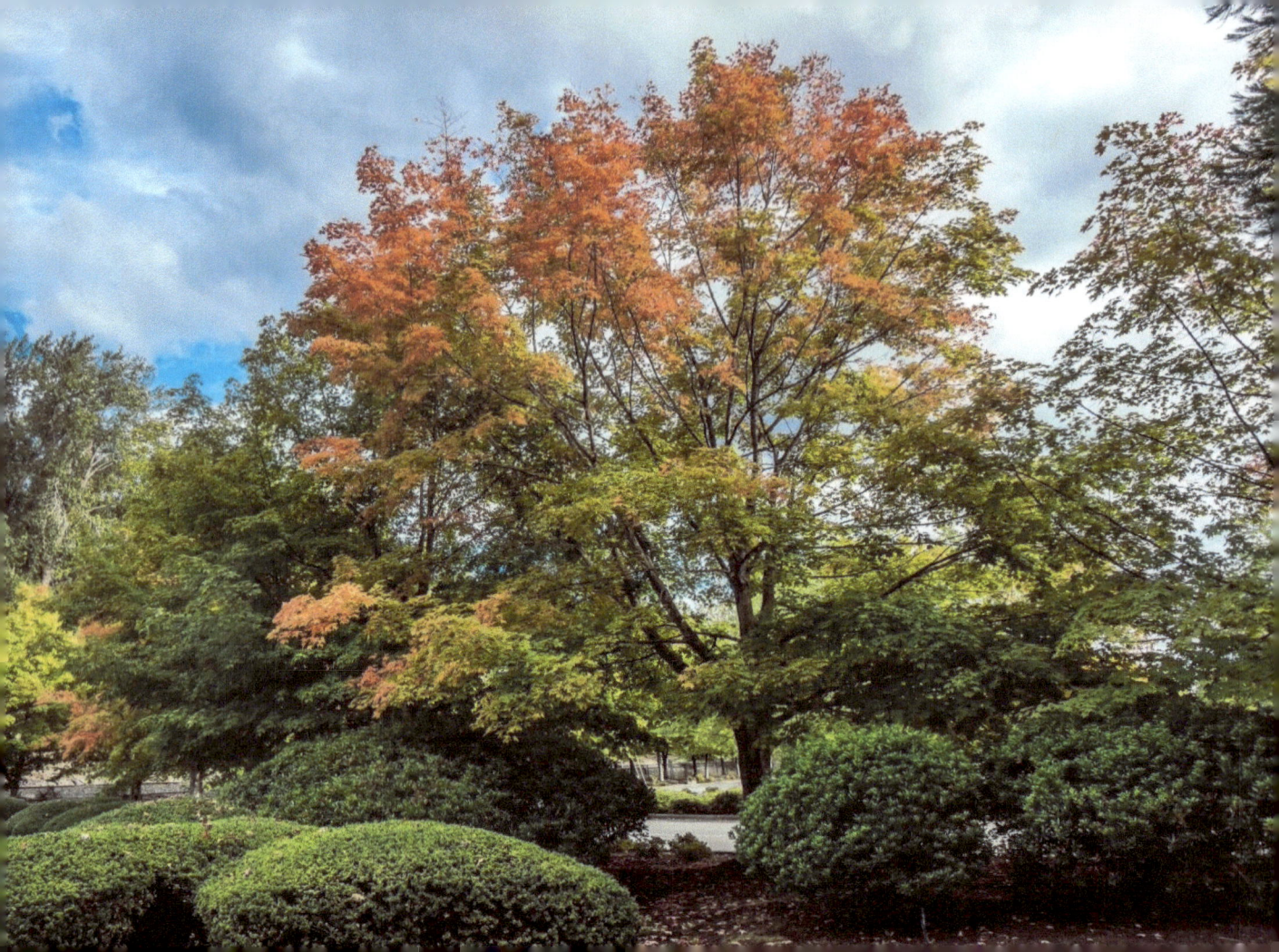

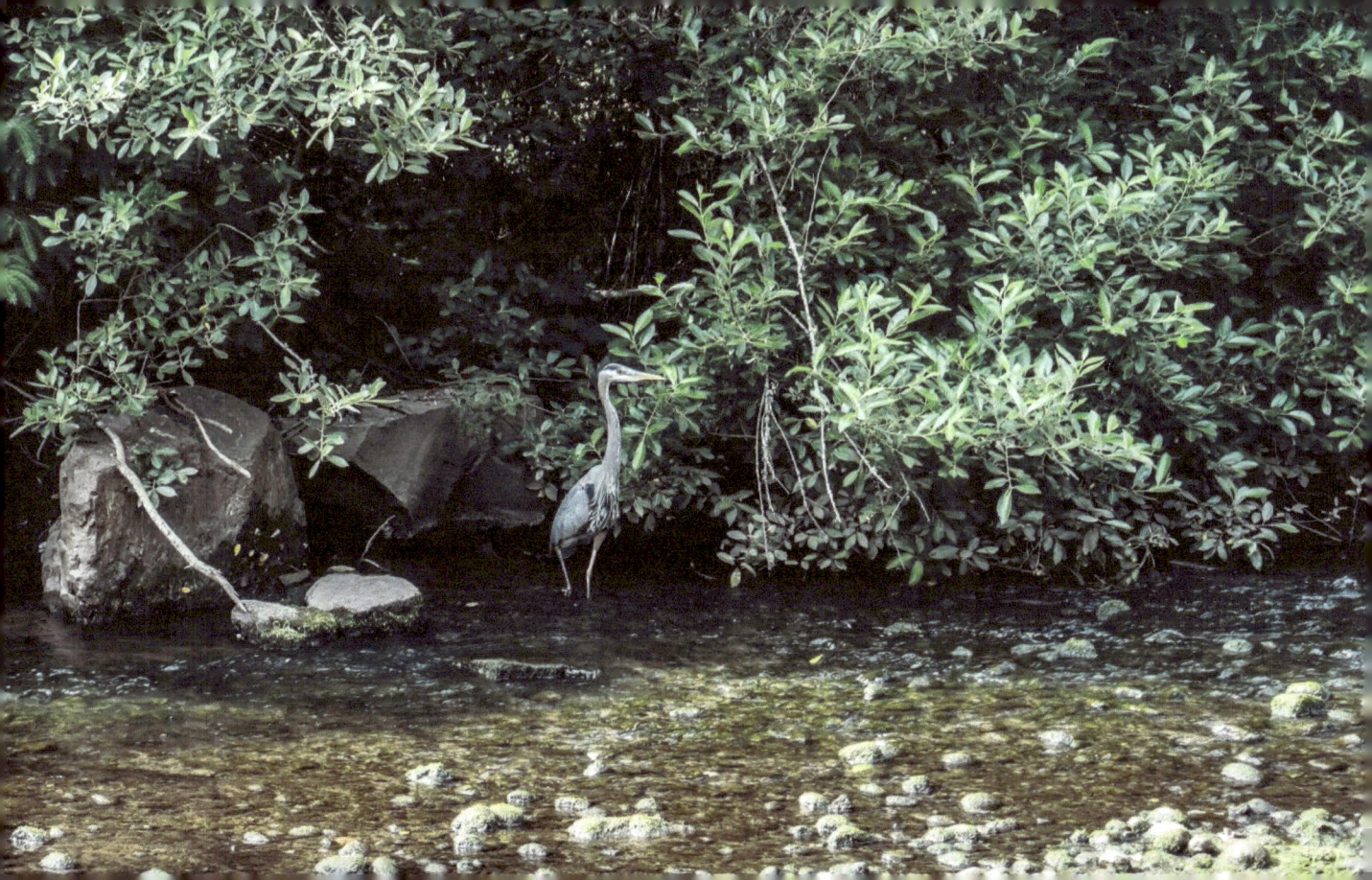

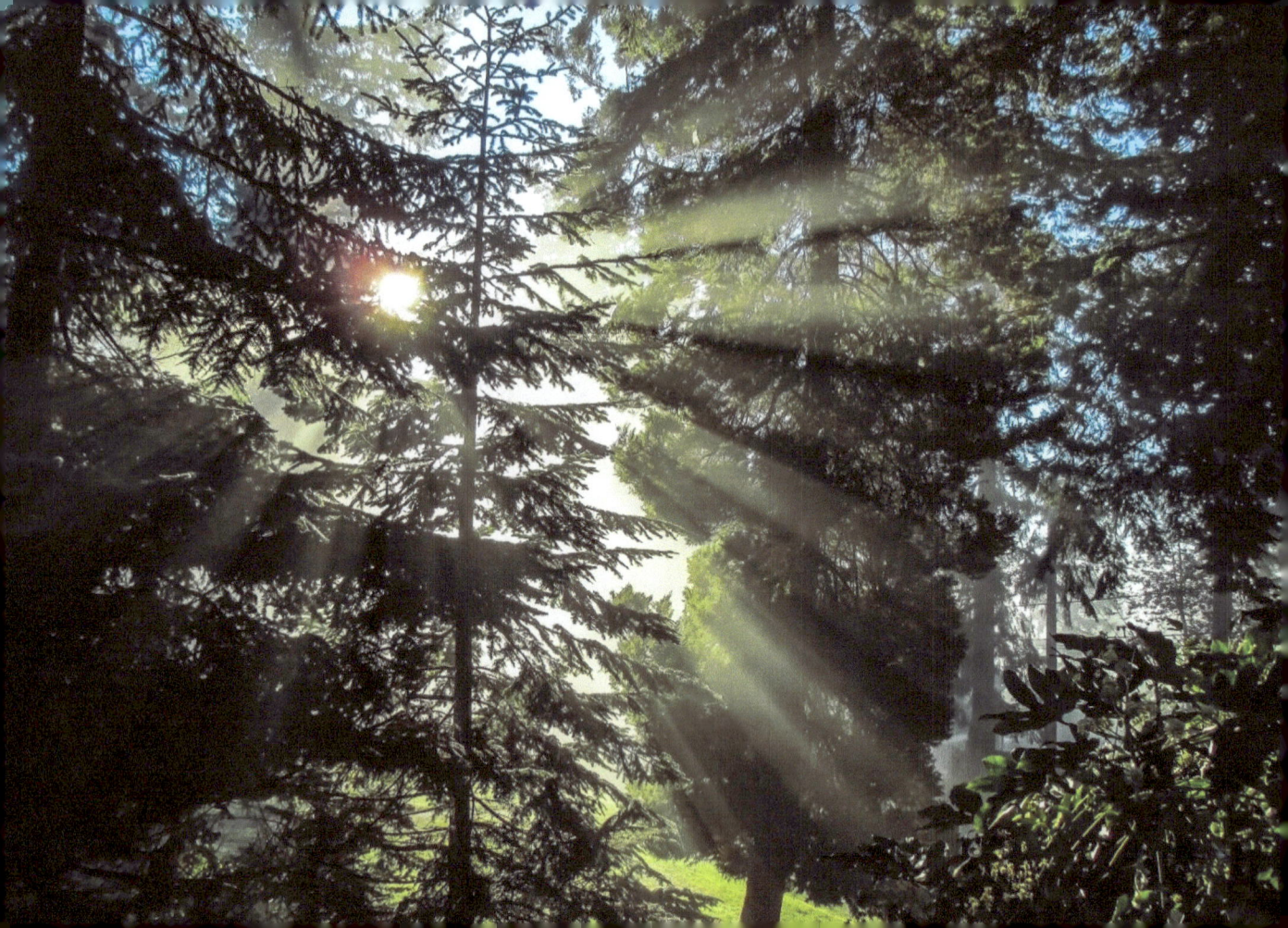

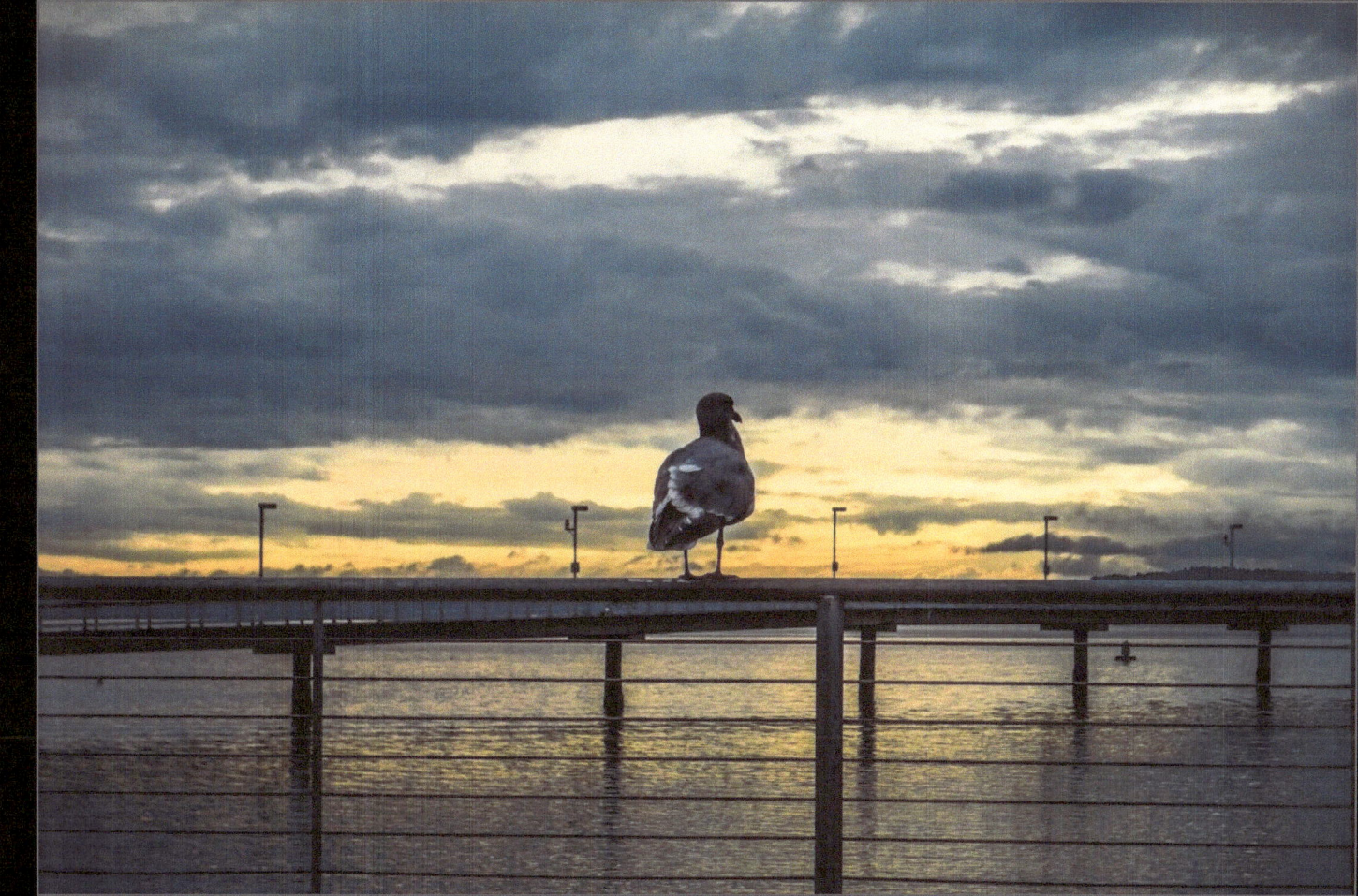

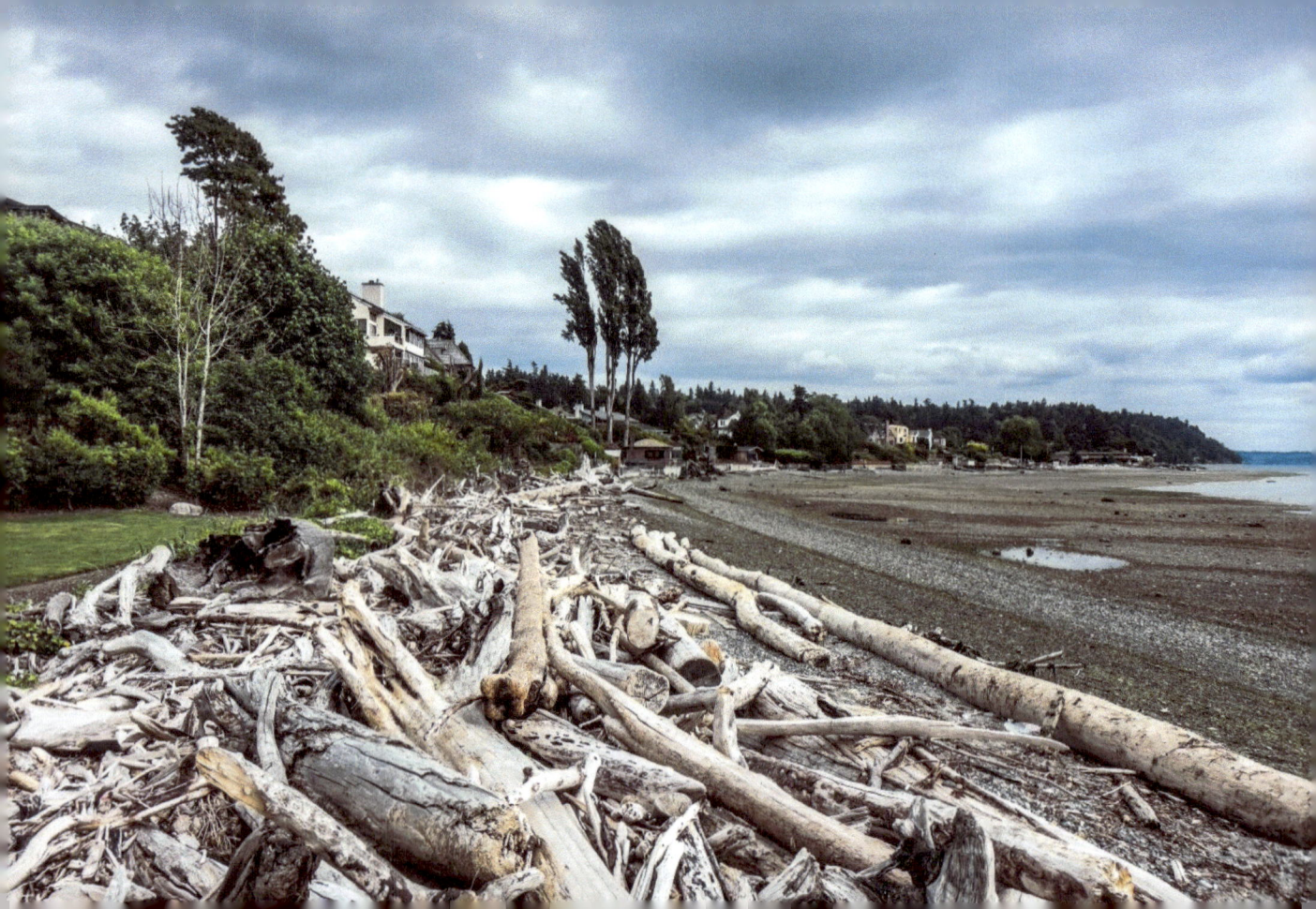

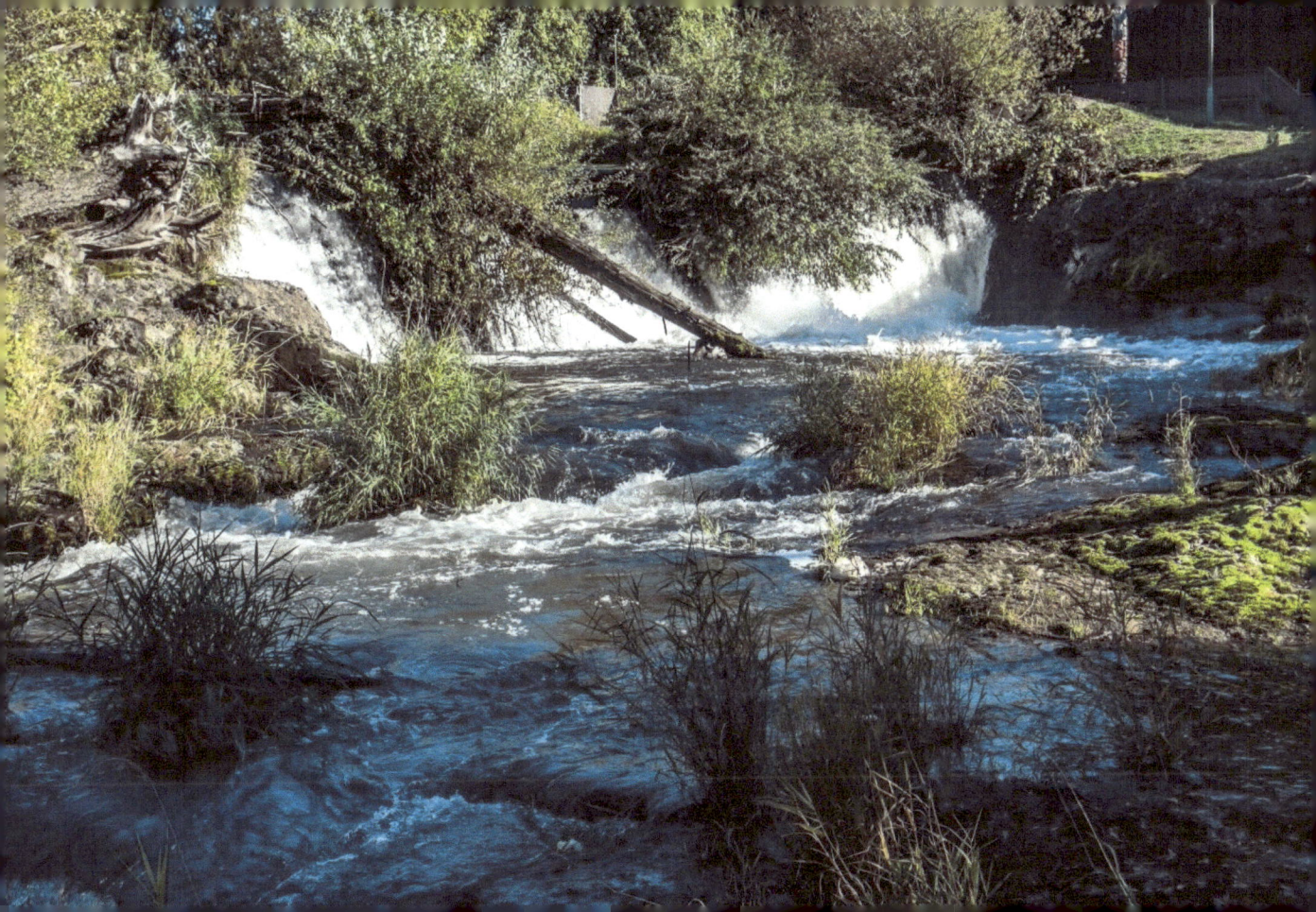

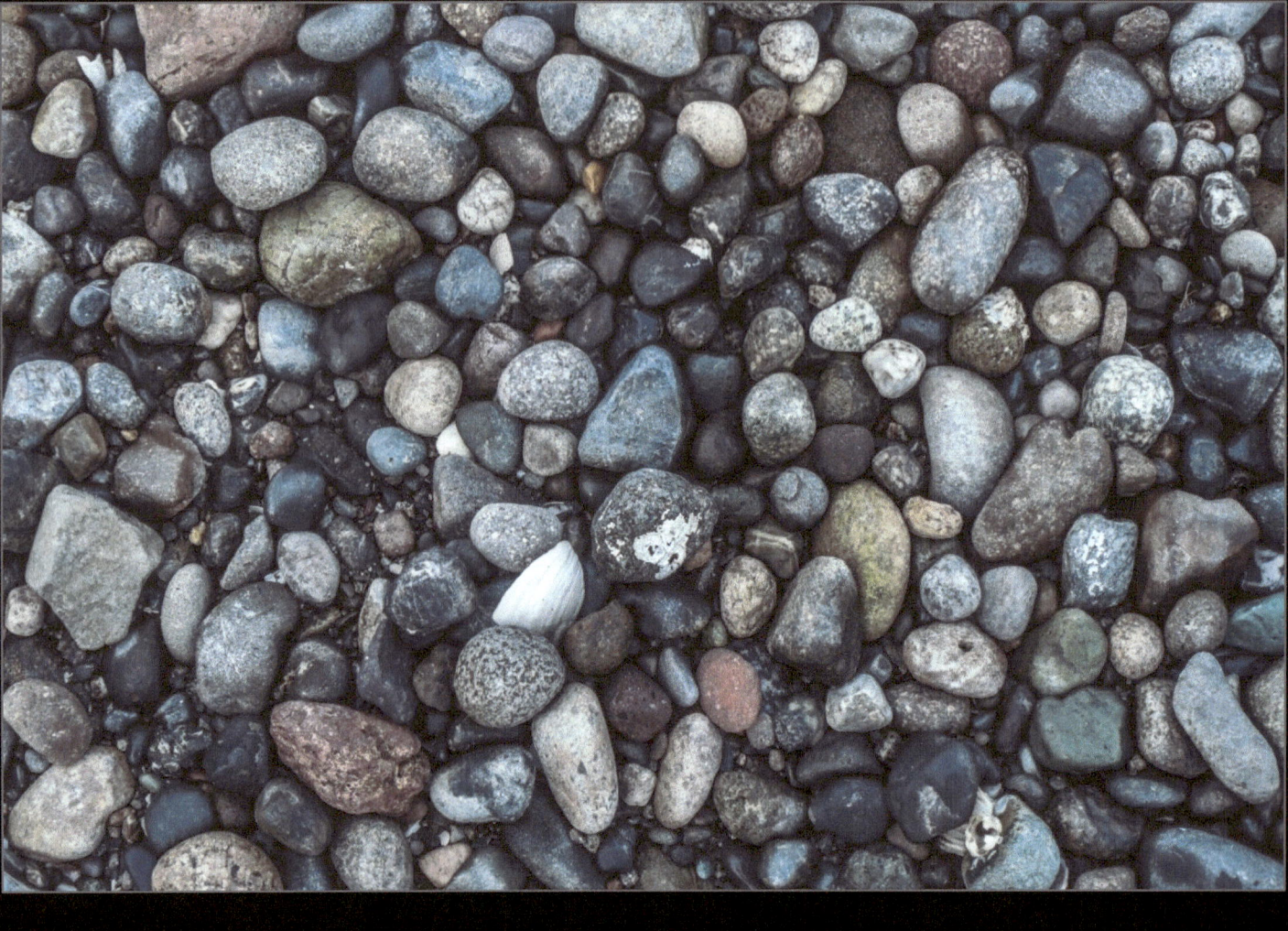

Rocks of various colors sit on water's
edge somewhere in the Pacific

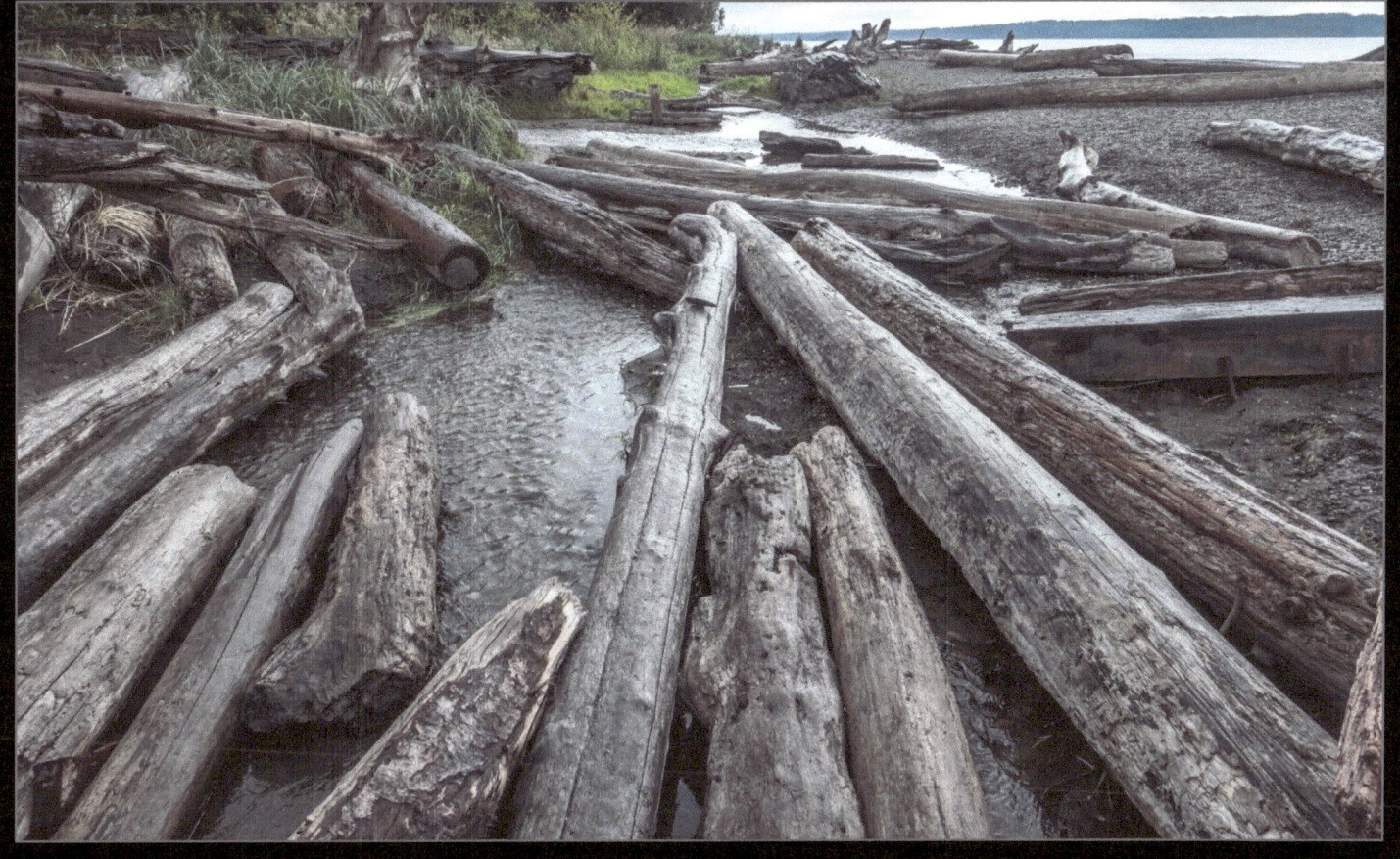

Close-up shot of driftwood logs at
Seahurst Beach Park in Burien,
Washington.

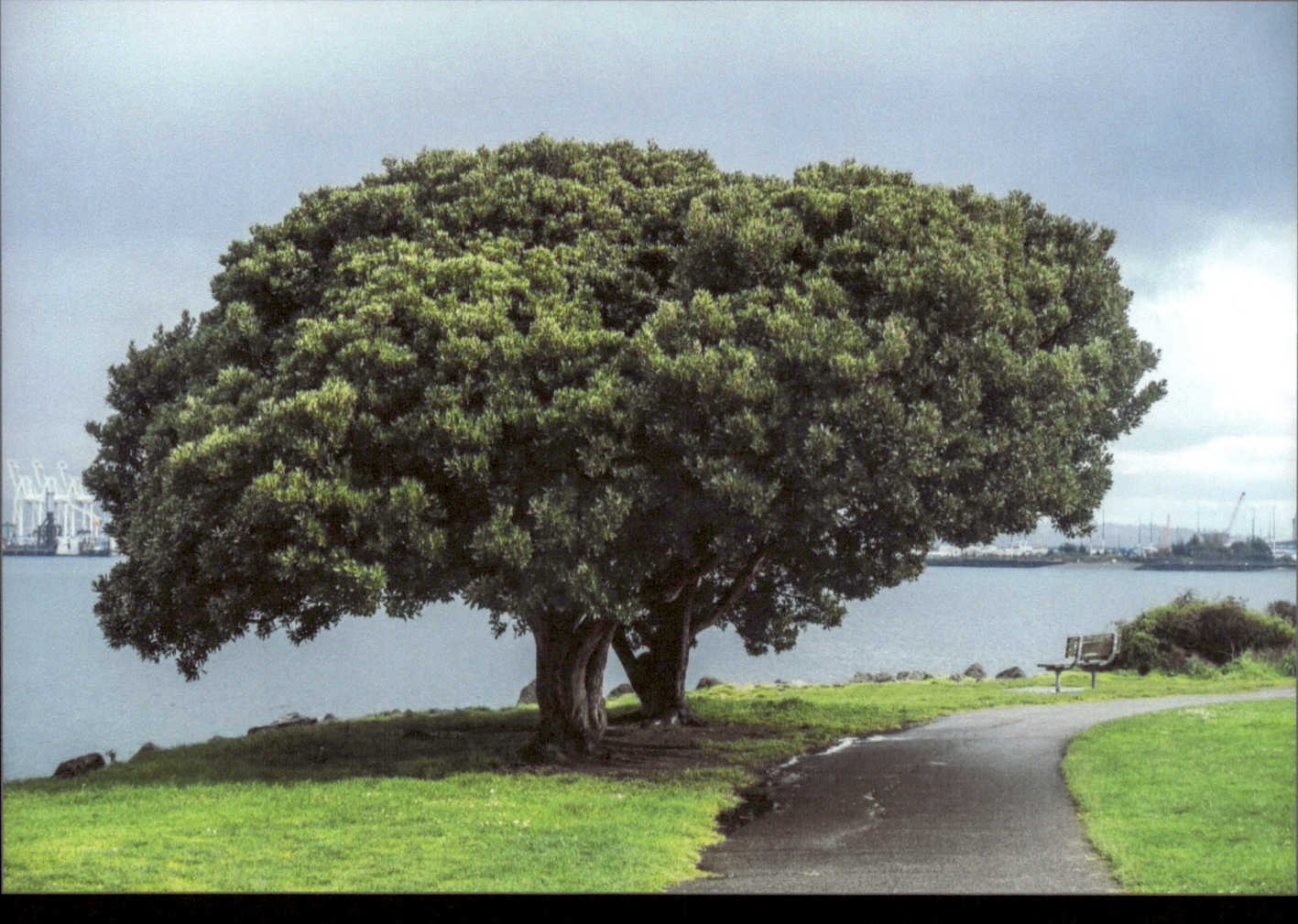

Two trees seem to merge into one.
Photo taken in West Seattle near Alki
Beach.

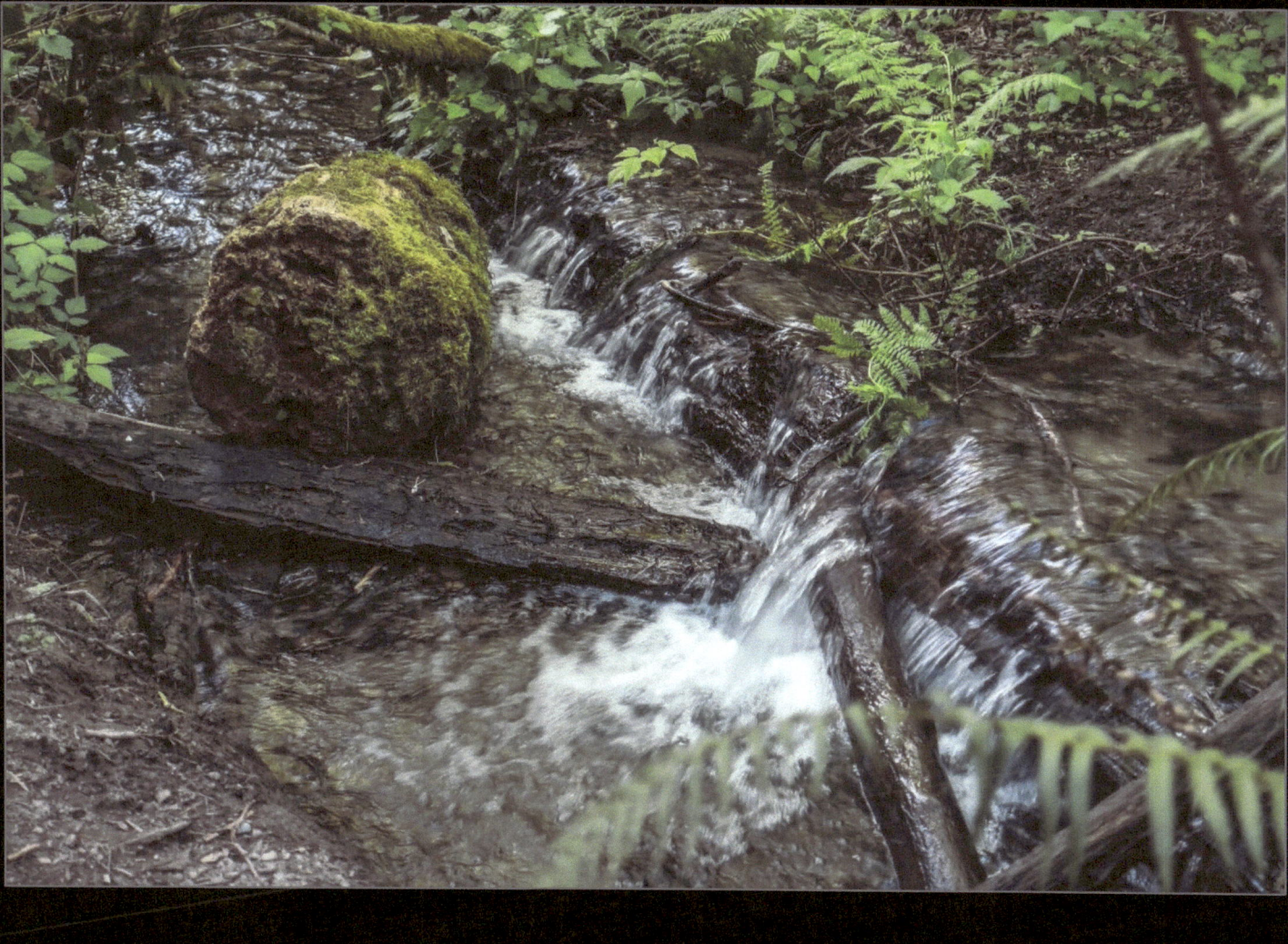

Water rushes over logs in a stream along the
trail at Dash Point State Park in Dash Point,

About The Author

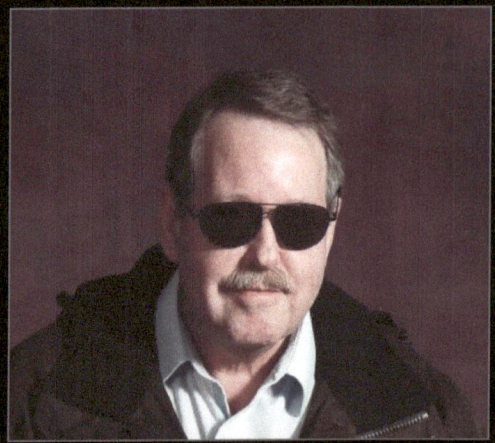

After writing four YA novels George
Matthew Cole discovered his
true passion in photography. He enjoys
taking photos near his home in the Pacific
Northwest with it's multitude of photo
opportunities. This is his first published
photography book.

Please send email to
georgecolephoto@georgemcole.com

Please visit his web site at
http://www.georgemcole.com

ISBN-13: 978-1539842965
ISBN-10: 1539842967

Find more information about the author
and his books at his web site.

http://www.georgemcole.com

Contact the author by email at:

georgecolephoto@georgemcole.com

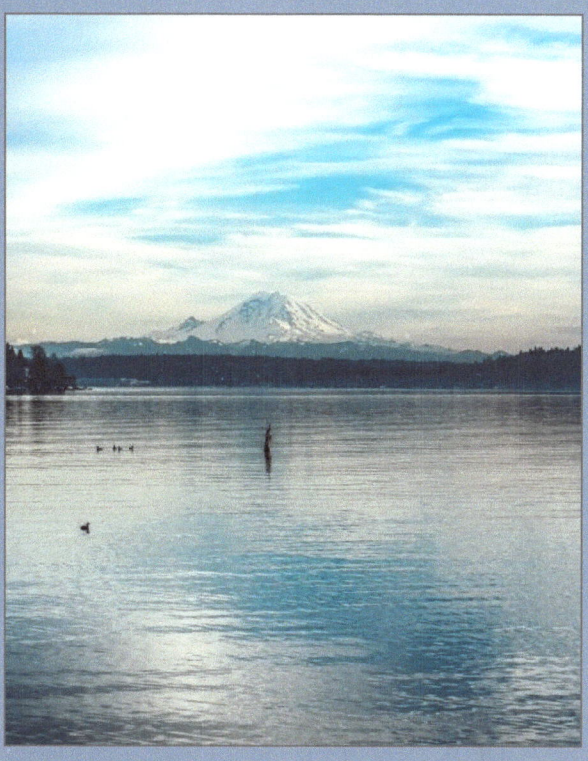

My special thanks to Jeannie and Alan Wolfe
for their ongoing support and suggestions.

www.ingramcontent.com/pod-product-compliance
Lightning Source LLC
Chambersburg PA
CBHW050836180526

45159CB00004B/1927